Plain Talk About Art

by
N. E. Lahti

PLAIN TALK ABOUT ART

First Printing: October, 1988

Library of Congress Catalog Card No. 88-050220

ISBN 0-9620147-0-2

YORK BOOKS

P.O. Box 40-1112, Brooklyn, New York 11240-1112

LIFE WITHOUT ART IS DEATH.
(Vita sine ars mors est.)

CONTENTS

Preface

This book grew out of a desire to recognize the words used by lecturers during art appreciation courses. I began to make a list of art terms. That list grew over a year's time to include art movements, historical eras and cultures of civilizations.

In studying this vast field, however, I discovered that many authoritative writings contained such esoteric language that comprehension was difficult. I began to dig deeper until I was able to interpret and translate into Plain English definitions of art terms, descriptions and aims of art movements, cultural ages known for their styles of art, and so forth.

Soon it became evident to me that there existed a need for a reference book that would contain understandable language for the lay person, especially since more and more of the general public are showing an interest in art.

My central motive in writing this book, therefore, is to communicate to those persons who would like to know more about art that language need not be a barrier to understanding. My secondary motive is to present a book that is affordable and easy to carry.

N. E. Lahti

Introduction by N. E. Lahti

The writer's purpose in writing PLAIN TALK ABOUT ART is to set out and clarify the words commonly used in the world of art, with Plain English as its vehicle.

The most well known and influential movements in art of the Western world and their outgrowths are described as succinctly as possible without overwhelming the reader with esoteric references. Names of artists belonging to movements or who created art in similar styles are also included. Brief essays on art from several parts of the world or from centuries past are given with a bird's-eye view to history. Accuracy, of course, is paramount, although in many instances it was noted that art historians differ in opinion or in their references. For example, the exact years for the commencement or conclusion of cultural ages, periods of art movements or the birth/death dates of artists may vary and names of art movements are occasionally interpreted from different viewpoints.

Artists named in the respective schools or movements are only representative of artists that are actually known to have been living at the same times or in the same regions or countries or who painted in a manner that expressed the style or the intentions of a particular group.

References to other cultural ages or art movements placed at the ends of descriptions are meant to guide the reader to the ensuing cultural age, the next movement in time, a contemporary movement or one that has some connection to it. Several individual art styles are also mentioned to give insight into the innovative methods or devices of the named artists.

Basically, this book is intended for easy alphabetical reference for the student of art appreciation. It is not an encyclopedia, a history book or a technical textbook. It is hoped, however, that its perusal will lead to a deeper study of art.

Because color is one of the most important aspects of art, a color vocabulary is appended. Although most of the words mentioned are found in everyday English, they will assist the spectator to view painting with an appreciation for color and to understand the terminology of critiques.

Abstract Art

Several of its principal motifs are:

1. The reduction of everything to concrete, essential form.
2. The theory that color and form have their own qualities.
3. The absence of reality.
4. Nonrepresentational imagery.
5. Penetration into the world of mystery to discover the basic truths of life.
6. Exploration of the fourth dimension through a higher consciousness.
7. A field of action.
8. A zone of silence.
9. The use of neoprimitive signs of the Native American culture.

Two major divisions exist:

A. Abstract Expressionism—A painterly, soft-edge style. Spontaneity is its primary source of expression. Brushwork often appears dynamic and aggressive. Shapes and colors are often used as symbols. See Abstract Expressionism.

B. Geometric Abstraction—A linear, hard-edge style. In essence, it is totally impersonal and marked by clarity and precision. Color is often used to emphasize structure. See Geometric Abstraction.

Kandinsky (1866–1944), the author of "Concerning the Spiritual in Art" (1912), is recognized as the first to establish Abstract Art as a unified and authentic style of expression. It was his wish to elevate the human spirit by dematerializing representational objects into symbols in the belief that pure form and pure color would make "sounds" that would reverberate into the soul. See Improvisations.

Abstract Collage

The application of materials retrieved from urban waste (cork, nails, rags, string, etc.) combined with painting of nonfigurative forms. Schwitters (1887–1948) is known for this art form. He called his productions "Merz."

Abstract-Creation (Art Nonfiguratif) (1931–1936)

A nonfigurative painting and sculptural movement founded to reflect the ideals of Abstract Art through three-dimensional form. Its primary intention was to encourage creative Geometric Abstraction in all forms. At one time it had over 400 adherents.

Abstract Expressionism a/k/a The New York School (1940s–1960s)

A school that changed the direction of Western painting: the art of painting seemed to be re-invented. Between 1942 and 1946 the modern art gallery and museum, Art of this Century, owned by Peggy Guggenheim, gave one-man exhibitions of the work of Pollock, Hofmann, Baziotes and others; it was during this time that Abstract Expressionism was launched.

DeKooning and Pollock are credited with being its most powerful influences. Among the so-called "first generation" were Hofmann (1880–1966); Tomlin (1899–1953); Rothko (1903–1970); Gottlieb (1903–1974); Gorky (1904–1948); Still (1904–1980); deKooning (b. 1904); Newman (1905–1970); Krasner (1908–1984); Kline (1910–1962); Pollock (1912–1956); Baziotes (1912–1963); Guston (1913–1980); Motherwell (b. 1915); Pousette-Dart (b. 1916), as well as artists in the Color Field school. "Second generation" artists include Bluhm (b. 1920); Hartigan (b. 1922); Goldberg (b. 1924); Mitchell (b. 1926); among others. See **Abstract Art, Action Painting, Drip Painting, Stain Painting** and **Art Informel.**

Abstractscapes

A term coined by McNeil (b. 1908) to describe his representations of nature which are abstracted into color daydreams.

Academic

A style following established rules.

Academy Art or Academic Tradition (Beaux-Arts)

Marked by traditional draftsmanship, somber color, beauty along with classical, historical or mythological themes.

Academy of Art

A term taken from antiquity. It was thereafter used by informal groups of artists in the 1400s in Italy who met for discussions. Official academies were established in Rome and Florence during the 1500s. The Royal Academy of Painting and Sculpture founded in Paris in 1649 established a strict regimen which set the pattern for future academies.

Acrylic Paint
A clear plastic used as a medium or as a vehicle for pigments.

Action Painting (1945–1955)
A technique unwittingly introduced by Wols (1913–1951) in his Surreal-like creations. The technique begins with the application of paint to a surface with unpremeditated movement, such as dripping, swirling or pouring, reflecting the artist's subconscious flow of action—when he lets things "happen." Pollock (1912–1956) used sticks, knives or trowels to apply paint that was mixed with sand, glass, etc. He compared himself to the Indian sand painters of the American West when he painted his unstretched canvas on the floor. It was Pollock's purpose to prove that paint had its own language. He was a strong influence on American painting.

Aesthetics
1. Referring to a philosophy applied to art in an attempt to understand its qualities.
2. The study of the beautiful in nature and art.

After
Referring to the style, copy or reproduction of a work of art. Occasionally, if a master artist's work became famous, his workshop would continue his style after his death. Leonard (b. 1933), an English portraitist, depicts his subjects after the style of well known artists from centuries past, according to his interpretation of the subject's facial characteristics and according to certain timeless elements.

Airbrush
A relatively new tool similar to a spray gun, used most often by commercial artists. Its primary purpose is to produce smooth gradations of colors and tones.

Alla Prima or Au Premier Coup
A painting completed at one sitting, giving the impression of strength and spontaneity.

Allegorical Painting
Narrative art in symbolic form, a technique of ambiguity used

in literature as well. One of the most famous is "The Sacred Allegory" by Giovanni Bellini (1430–1516). Its meaning is still being debated. In more recent years, the work of Erlebacher (b. 1937) whose greatest influence has been Renaissance painting. Her nude figure compositions, similar to Biblical scenes, generally show men and women expressing their anguish over the human condition.

All-Over Painting
A term associated with large Abstract Expressionist paintings wherein paint was applied without plan. Also refers to the Color Field school.

Alternative Spaces a/k/a Artists' Spaces
In an effort to bypass the commercial gallery system, artists (mostly women) have formed co-op galleries. The primary purpose of the co-op movement is to provide a more democratic way to show work and to circulate ideas.

American Abstract Artists (1936–early 1940s)
An association formed in New York City that promoted and annually exhibited Abstract Art of every kind. Among its members were Knaths, Reinhardt, Albers, Pollock, deKooning and so on. They once picketed the Museum of Modern Art to demand that it show American art.

American Artists, Society of
This was established in 1877 by a group of 22 artists called "The New Movement" to provide a more democratic policy for the exhibition of art, based on merit, in reaction to the restrictive policies of the National Academy of Design. In 1898 a group called "The Ten" seceded. In 1906 the Society was reabsorbed by the National Academy.

American Art Union
Beginning in 1839 this organization distributed original art to 19,000 subscribers by lottery. It played a vital role in American art because it did much to bring genuine works of art to the people, whether by known or unknown artists. The union was dissolved in 1852 when the operation was declared illegal, but its success led to the establishment of smaller art unions.

American Gothic by Wood (1892–1942)

A famous classic American painting depicting a Midwestern farmer and his spinster daughter. This painting has been parodied many times by other artists.

American Impressionism

Referring to those artists who followed the Paris school. Borrowed characteristics were high-keyed and broken color, nonacademic technique, and the pleasant life. Perry (1848–1933); Chase (1849–1916); Tryon (1849–1925); Metcalf (1853–1925); Sargent (1856–1925); Vonnoh (1858–1933); Tarbell (1862–1938); Horton (1865–1936); Pages (1867–1946); Singer (1868–1943); Redfield (1869–1965); Rosen (1878–1950); among others. See **Giverny Group, New Hope School and The Ten.**

American Indian Art—See **North American Indian and Eskimo Art.**

American Landscape Painting

The creation of paintings to celebrate the landscape of North America. Luminism was a special quality used to enhance color of the natural world. Another quality was grandeur that seemed to reflect the growing nationalistic spirit of Americans who were in awe of the wilderness and its beauty. In recent decades, however, the tendency is to portray landscape more realistically. Guy (1760–1820); Fisher (1792–1863); Cole (1801–1848); Key (1832–1920); LaFarge (1835–1910); C. Rockwell (1837–1907); Welch (1844–1919); Blakelock (1847–1919); Clark (1848–1917); J. E. Stuart (1852–1941); Murphy (1853–1921); Coffin (1855–1925); Valencia (1856–1935); Albert (1857–1946); Sparks (1862–1937); Bogert (1864–1944); Gray (1869–1952); Carlson (1874–1945); White (1883–1969); Pleissner (1905–1983); Sloane (1905–1985); Fetherolf (b. 1925); Welliver (b. 1929); Timberlake (b. 1937); Downes (b. 1939); Maguire (b. 1940); Butler (b. 1945); Armstrong (b. 1947); among others. See **Hudson River School, Landscape, Marine Painting and Western and Indian Art.**

American Scene Painting (1920s–1940s)

The portrayal of American life in certain regions, urban life, human interest and industry.

Two major areas were covered: Social Realism and Regionalism.

Regionalists include Blumenschien (1874–1960); Ufer (1876–1936); Hartley (1877–1943); Kraft (1884–1938); Dunn (1884–1952); Hibbard (1886–1972); Benton (1889–1975); Wood (1892–1942); Burchfield (1893–1967); Curry (1897–1946); Hurd (1904–1984) and Bohrod (b. 1907). See **Regionalism**.

Social Realism is represented in the paintings of the so-called **Ashcan School** and the **14th Street School** as well as those artists referred to in **Social Realism**.

American School

Copley (1737–1815); Stuart (1755–1828); Allston (1779–1843); Audubon (1785–1851); Morse (1791–1872); Mount (1807–1868); Bingham (1811–1879); Fuller (1822–1884); Innes (1825–1894); Whistler (1834–1903); Homer (1836–1910); Eakins (1844–1916); Sargent (1856–1925); Marin (1870–1953); Sloan (1871–1951); Bellows (1882–1925); Benton (1889–1975); Wood (1892–1942); Marsh (1898–1954); A. Wyeth (b. 1917); Beal (b. 1931); J. Wyeth (b. 1946).

American Tonalism (1880–1910)

A school of American landscape painting. Like the Impressionists, the tonalists were primarily interested in expressing the mood of light and atmosphere in nature. They preferred, however, to paint the quiet times of days and seasons when the world presented only a limited scale of colors. Their strongest influence was Whistler (1834–1903). Keith (1839–1911); Smillie (1840–1921); B. Harrison (1845–1911); DeHaven (1856–1934); Appel (1857–1934); Eaton (1857–1934); Peters (1862–1928); Dabo (1868–1960); among others.

Anarchistic Synthesis

A movement consisting of two dissident Soviet artists, Komar (b. 1943) and Melamid (b. 1945), residing in the U.S. They specialize in disturbing satire and derision: political symbols and anti-social behavior are common themes. Appropriated images, styles and techniques are taken from the entire history of Western painting, especially 20th century art, and Soviet art. Several titles: "Yale Conference" (1982); "View of the Kremlin in a Romantic Landscape" (1981–1982); "Yalta" (1986–1987) consisting of 31 panels, each unique. The two artists work so closely that when one starts a painting, the other can finish it. They work in a mixed media and most of their work is multi-paneled.

Anatomy
The study and exploration of bone structure and musculature as well as the form and movement of the body.

Ancient Art
The art existing during pre-Christian years in the Near East and Mediterranean areas. For the Near East, see Egyptian Art and Mesopotamian Art. For the Mediterranean area, refer to Mediterranean Art subdivided by the Minoan Culture and the Mycenaean Culture.

Ancients, The
A group of English artists who gathered around Blake (1757–1827) and who painted with an imaginative vision with Biblical stories, allegory and poetical themes as their subjects. Blake believed himself to be under heavenly guidance and that it was the artist's duty to make his visions real to others. Linnel (1778–1842); Calvert (1799–1883); Palmer (1805–1881); among others.

Anti-Cerne
A white, black or colored outline.

Antiquity
Referring to the period of about 500 B.C. in Greece up to the years before the Middle Ages.

Antropofaunas
An art form peculiar to Millares (1926–1972) whereby he created a series of paintings using red painted rags, rough textiles, scribbled forms, etc. as his contents.

Applied Art
Art that is applied to the design and decoration of useful objects and to lettering and illustration, and an attempt to unite the aesthetics of the fine arts therewith. Commercial art is considered a branch of Applied art. See Industrial Art.

Applique
A cut-out applied to a larger piece of material.

Appropriated
Referring to work relying on well-known images. See Derivative and Eclecticism.

Aquarelle
The use of transparent watercolors.

Arabesque
A curvilinear, rhythmic, decorative pattern of interwoven lines. Outlines of flowers, fruit, animals, etc. are often used.

Arcadian Art
A scene depicting simple pleasure and quiet. The contemplation of pleasure in nature was broadened by 19th century idealized art.

Archipentura
A title given by Archipenko (1887–1964) to his invention of a machine (1924) for the showing of paintings in motion.

Architectonic
A style seeming to have been derived from architectural form.

Architectons
A name given to the three-dimensional abstract architectural forms of Malevich (1878–1935). See Constructivism.

Architecture
1. The art or science of designing and building structures.
2. The art of shaping space to meet human needs.

Armory Show, The (1913)
A well-known international exhibition, formally called the International Exhibition of Art, given in New York City to exhibit "the works of progressive and live painters, both American and foreign. . . ." The work of Duchamp, Goya, Ingres, Delacroix, Cezanne, van Gogh and many others was shown along with that of American artists Whistler, Hassam, Ryder, The Eight and so on.

Arrangement
1. The making of something by placing its parts together.

2. The placing of shapes and colors upon a flat surface for aesthetic purposes.

Art and its various definitions:

1. A method of instruction through delight. (Greek)
2. That which instructs, arouses pious emotions and awakens memories. (St. Bonaventura)
3. Painting is a science and should be pursued as an enquiry into the laws of Nature. (Constable)
4. . . . the outward expression of an inner need. (Kandinsky)
5. What I dream of is an art of balance, of purity and serenity. . . . (Matisse)
6. . . . exactitude winged by intuition. (Klee)
7. A picture . . . is essentially a flat surface covered with colors assembled in a certain order. (Denis)
8. There is no such thing as art. There are only artists. (Gombrich)
9. Organized perception is what art is all about. (Lichtenstein)

Art Brut

A style formulated from primitive, lunatic or children's art which Dubuffet (1901–1985) cultivated in a highly sophisticated manner. Wolfli (1864–1930); Hernandez (1893–1957); Carlo (b. 1916); Duf (b. 1920); Demkin (b. 1929); among others.

Art Critic

One who engages in the analysis and evaluation of art. It involves knowledge of the liberal arts, specifically literature and philosophy.

Art Dealer

One who deals in art and supports and promotes the work of artists in an attempt to sell it.

Art Deco (1920s–1930s)

A popular international decorative and architectural style marked by a modern, streamlined look and bold, rhythmic, geometric forms, such as zigzags, triangles, stripes, circles and spires. It was the pervasive architectural style in midtown Manhattan, New York City: the Chrysler Building, the Empire State Building and Rockefeller Center remain as its most well known buildings. Utilitarian objects adapted to this style include furniture, clocks, lamps, rugs, wallpaper, and ceramics, in addition to the Graphic Arts. Currently it seems to be making a small comeback.

Art Engagé

Referring to art with political or social meaning.

Arte Povera (1970s)

This involved two Italian movements:

1. A reaction against traditional art with Happenings as the primary source of creation in the artist's attempt to interpret reality.
2. The creation of art from rough and worthless materials. Burri (b. 1915); Tapies (b. 1924); Pistoletto (b. 1933); Ceroli (b. 1938); among others.

Art Film

After World War II themes of films changed to reflect a more realistic character in contrast to Hollywood's world of fantasy and make-believe.

Art for Art's Sake

The theory that art exists for the creation of beauty alone. Forms, colors, lines, space, etc. are arranged for their own sake rather than for content.

Art Form

A recognized form of artistic expression.

Artful

Showing art skill.

Art Gallery

A place where works of art are sold for profit. The principal activity of the owner is to establish the importance of the artists chosen and represented by the gallery through advertising, openings, etc. as ways of attracting critics and curators and to inspire the confidence of collectors to purchase the art. See Alternative Spaces.

Art Guild—See Guild.

Art Historian

1. A student of art history.
2. A writer of books or articles, who is generally considered an expert.
3. One who is steeped in the knowledge of art.

Art History

Concerning a lifetime of learning in the liberal arts. It offers a rich and varied knowledge and broadens the experience of those who perceive it.

Articulation

The manner in which adjacent shapes or forms join—a technique that varies with each painter.

Artifact

1. A simple object showing workmanship.
2. A product of artistic endeavor.

Art Informel (Art without form; free abstraction) (1940s–1950s)

An important European (especially Spanish) school after World War II which corresponded with the New York School of Abstract Expressionism in its use of cryptic symbols and color compositions. It was a spontaneous, undisciplined art which gave expression to the fantasy of an "obscure half world." Occasionally, it was referred to as "un art autre" (another art). Generally, it included:

1. Expressive Abstraction with spontaneity as its motif. Permeke (1886–1952); Hartung (b. 1904); Wols (1913–1951); Soulages (b. 1919); Mathieu (b. 1921); Saez (b. 1925); Vento (b. 1925); Cardenas (b. 1928); Turios (b. 1933); among others. See El Paso.

2. Tachisme (Action Painting). Bissiere (1888–1964); Lanskoy (1902–1976); Esteve (b. 1904); Atlan (1913–1960); deStael (1914–1955); Guerrero (b. 1914); B. Schultze (b. 1915); Saura (b. 1930); among others.
3. Abstract Lyrique. Afro (1912–1976); Schumacher (b. 1912); Unger (b. 1915); Dufour (b. 1922); Stamos (b. 1922); Gillet (b. 1924); Arnal (b. 1924); Rezvani (b. 1928); Kallos (b. 1928); among others. See Lyrical Abstraction.

Its sculptors include Kemeny (1907–1965); Chillida (b. 1924); A. Pomodoro (b. 1926); G. Pomodoro (b. 1930); among others.

Artisan

One who possesses manual dexterity or skill: a craftsperson.

Artist

1. A person who is skilled in one of the fine arts.
2. The creator of composite images.
3. He/she enlarges our perception and increases our knowledge of the realities and potential values of the world.

Artistry

The artistic quality of workmanship.

Artist's Proof a/k/a/ A/P

One or more proofs of a limited edition of prints. They are made for the artist's use for specific purposes, such as correction or addition. Signed, but un-numbered proofs, usually the first 10 percent, are occasionally sold.

Art=Language

A reactionary movement by Conceptual artists against the intellectualized writings of art magazines.

Artless

Crude: the lack of art or skill.

Art Mobilier

The carvings and decorated objects found on pre-historic sites.

Art Movement

An informal group of artists who work together for practical as well as ideological purposes. In some instances, they have shared workshops and materials and published periodicals or books. Movements usually last no longer than five years because members leave to form other groups or they change their style. At times, artists will be designated as belonging to a certain movement based on the timing of their recognition.

Art Nouveau (1890s–1905)

An international luxury style in design emerging from the Symbolist movement. It was marked by curvilinear pattern and flowing line and was generally applicable to ceramics, furniture, jewelry, posters, typography, sculpture and painting. It was also referred to as the New Art, the 1900 Style and the Modern Style. In Germany it was known as Jugendstil; in Italy as Stile Liberty; in Barcelona, Modernistica became the pervasive style. Contributing artists were Galle (1846–1904); Mucha (1860–1933); Horta (1861–1947); Klimt (1862–1918); Beardsley (1872–1898); Gaudi (1882–1926).

Art Patron

A wealthy or influential supporter of an artist or of the fine arts.

Art Period

A certain age which produces art possessing similar characteristics. An artist usually expresses the time in which he lives. The major divisions are:

Ancient, noted for sculpture
Medieval, noted for architecture
Modern, noted for painting

Arts and Crafts Movement (1875–1920)

An English but eventually international reactionary movement against the standardizing effects of the machine and mass production, inspired by Wm. Morris (1834–1896), a writer and a designer. A call was made for the return to handcraftsmanship and simplicity along with the plea of "joy in labor." It wanted to combine all creative and semi-creative work. In the U.S. the call was so strong that communities and societies were established and books and magazines published to promote a back-to-basics philosophy in design.

Art Students League of New York

A school organized in 1875 for the purpose of teaching drawing and sketching. It has no set courses of studies or other requirements. It has enjoyed success through the years and has attracted many distinguished teachers to its staff. A large number of its former students have become well-known artists.

Art Therapy

A free form of art used to relieve patients of stress.

Arty

Pretentiously artistic.

Ashcan School (sometimes referred to as the Revolutionary Black Gang) (1900s–1930s)

The first American movement of the 20th century consisting of a group of five American Realist painters (Henri, Lawson, Bellows, Luks and Sloan) who had exhibited with The Eight. They painted pictures based on the human interest angle with emphasis on urban life. They have been more accurately called the New York Realists. See **14th Street School.**

Assemblage

A term coined by Duchamp to describe the integration of art with ready-mades or found objects. It is an art form that exists somewhere between painting and sculpture wherein art is created from pre-existing elements: the artist's contribution would be in knowing how to assemble them. Nevelson (1899–1988); Cornell (1903–1973); Rauschenberg (b. 1925); Trova (b. 1927); Chamberlain (b. 1927) Kienholz (b. 1927); Marisol (b. 1930); Johns (b. 1930); Dine (b. 1935); among others. See **Environments/Assemblages, Junk Art** and **Sculpture** and **Sculptured Wall.**

Asymmetry

1. Dissimilar proportions are brought into balance.
2. Lacking a clear, definite center of interest.

Atelier

1. An artist's or craftsperson's workshop.
2. A studio where an artist trains students or where assistants work under the artist's supervision.

Athenaeum, The
The world-renowned portrait of George Washington by Stuart (1755–1828).

Attribute
A conventional, symbolic object used for identifying a meaning, such as a dog for fidelity.

Attribution, Attributed To
The assignment of a work of art to a certain artist or school based on style or documentary evidence.

Audio Installation Art (1970s–1980s)
The use of computer and audio technology within a tableau or setting whereby the interaction between the atmosphere and the environment becomes "visible": a sophisticated kinetic sculpture transformed into sound through a physical act, such as touch or movement. Cage (b. 1912); D. Oppenheim (b. 1938); Acconci (b. 1940); Monk (b. 1942); Lucier (b. 1944); Fontana (b. 1947); Phillips (b. 1951); among others. See **Video Art.**

Audiokinetic Sculpture
Sculpture whereby lights, sounds, music, moving parts, labyrinths, mirrors are combined to give the effect of a sculpture funhouse. Schoffer (b. 1912); Rhoads (b. 1926); Morellet (b. 1926); le Parc (b. 1928); among others. See **Sculpto-Pictoramas and Pseudomachines.**

Auto-Destruction Art—See DIAS.

Automatic Drawing
A technique practiced by Kelly (b. 1923) whereby he allowed ink to run down a page and then guided it by blowing on the ink. He wanted to get rid of preconceived ideas about art.

Automatism
A Surreal technique of creation: the release of subconscious images; free association (as in doodling) and intuition; the expression of deep and basic emotions. Automatism was central to the theme of Surrealism. Picasso used the phrase "voyage of discovery."

Avant-Garde

An intellectual group that develops unconventional or experimental concepts. The artist is a precursor to future art, in contrast to traditional concentration on the past.

Aviation and Space Art

The creation of paintings depicting the age of flight and space travel. Many of the images have been recorded by the aviators and astronauts themselves. Artists of this genre have realistically portrayed man's visual experience with the universe as well as the history of early flights, technological advances and the conquest of space. Famous air battles have also been recorded. McCall (b. 1919); Coulson (b. 1926); Bean (b. 1932); Christensen (b. 1942); W. Phillips (b. 1945); Kodera (b. 1956); among others.

Background

That part of a painting which lies behind objects in the foreground.

Bad Painting a/k/a/ The Wild Ones or Transavantgardes (late 1970s–1980s)

An international movement deliberately depicting art and sculpture in a crude and stylistic manner. Baselitz (b. 1938); Kiefer (b. 1945); Chia (b. 1946); Aycock (b. 1946); Fetting (b. 1949); Schnabel (b. 1951); Clemente (b. 1952); among others. See Neo-Expressionism.

Bambocciani (1630s–late 1600s)

A group of artists in Rome who depicted subjects from peasant and gypsy life as well as from a low class of society. A number of Flemish artists followed this trend.

Barbarian Art

The term Barbarian was applied by Greeks and Romans to persons outside their own culture. The art of wandering tribes in Europe, Asia and Africa was diverse and lively with a sense of beauty and much skill. Endemic to nomadic living was the decoration of tents, weapons, jewelry, metalwork and precious stones. Their strong feeling for design, decoration and bright colors influenced the medieval arts of sculpture, architecture and manuscript painting.

Barbizon School (1830s–1880s)

A group of French artists whose visual approach to painting planted the seed for Impressionism. They made the important decision to paint out-of-doors, although completion of their paintings may have been done in the studio. Corot (1796–1875); Diaz (1808–1876); Tryon (1810–1865); T. Rousseau (1812–1867); Millet (1814–1875); Daubigney (1817–1878); among others. Impressionists Monet, Pissarro and Sisley were strongly influenced by Corot. See Macchiaioli School.

Baroque (1590–1730)

A style of art, sculpture and architecture born in Rome. Although it took on diverse forms in several countries, it was the predominant style in Europe of that time. Baroque was a direct outgrowth of Mannerism and was marked by excessive light/shade, rich ornamentation, emotionalism, illusion and an increased use of color. Essentially, Baroque produced scenarios in which drama was presented within the forms of architecture, painting and sculpture.

Bernini (1598–1680), a painter, sculptor and architect, is recognized as its dominant force. He worked on various projects at St. Peter's Church for over 40 years; his "The Ecstacy of St. Teresa" is classic of Baroque. L. Carracci (1555–1619); Caravaggio (1569–1609); Guercino (1591–1666); Carriera (1675–1757); Tiepolo (1696–1770).

Rubens (1577–1640), a Flemish painter, caused its popularity to grow on an international scale. He was the first painter to develop Baroque movement.

By the 1600s, the Netherlands had split into two religious groups. In the Northern Protestant part, art became restricted to non-religious subjects, such as portraiture, genre, still-life and marine-and-landscape. (Those artists who were not portraitists could no longer depend on commissions, but instead painted pictures in the hope of attracting buyers.) It was discovered at this time that great paintings could be created from commonplace subject matter, especially in still-life. Hals (1580–1666); Rembrandt (1606–1669); Steen (1626–1679); van Ruisdael (1628–1682); Vermeer (1632–1675); among others.

French Baroque (a/k/a/ Baroque Classicism) was reflected mainly in its architecture during the reign of Louis XIV. During the Age of Versailles, Paris replaced Rome as the center of pictorial arts. La Tour (1593–1652); Poussin (1594–1665), the "father" of French art; Claude Lorrain (1600–1682); among others.

Spanish Baroque is seen in the work of de Ribera (1588–1652); Zurbaran (1598–1664); Velasquez (1599–1660); Murillo (1617–1682). See Rococo.

Bateau-Lavoir Group

A discussion group consisting of the first followers of Cubism in Paris in 1908. Among its artist members were Picabia (1879–1953); Gleizes (1881–1953); Metzinger (1883–1956); La Fresnaye (1885–1925); Delaunay (1885–1941); among others. See Puteau Group.

Bauhaus

A school formed by Gropius (1883–1969) in Germany in 1919 to eliminate the distinction between the fine arts and the applied arts. Its motto was "Form follows function." Rules were promulgated for a well-ordered style of painting in abstract form with a minimalist aesthetic. The Bauhaus became a symbol for creative construction and revolutionized the practice of art and design. Its influence on industrial design was profound and many Bauhaus products became prototypes for mass-produced items. Staff members were Albers, Klee and Kandinsky in the pictorial arts; Moholy-Nagy in photography; Schlemmer in theatre; Bayer in graphics; Gropius, van der Rohe and Meyer in architecture. When the school was closed by the Nazis in 1933, many of its teachers migrated to the U.S. and re-established a school in Chicago in 1937, which became the Institute of Design.

Baxter Prints

A printing process perfected by Baxter (1804–1867) whose reproductions were noted for their color, perspective and accuracy. They were quite comparable to oil paintings. See **Le Blond Ovals.**

Bay Area Figuration a/k/a/ California Figurative Painters (1940s)

They depicted scenes of domestic intimacy or community life with ideas from old paintings applied to contemporary art. Extravagant colors and large brushstrokes were their vehicles. Park (1911–1960); Bischoff (b. 1916); Diebenkorn (b. 1922); among others.

Beaux-Arts—See Academy Art.

Bella Maniera

The highest expression of an age.

Bella Peinture, La

1. The tradition of an artist whose pleasure in painting lies in the craft, material and technique.
2. A highly accomplished type of painting that employs all the painting skills.

Bergeries

Pictures of landscapes, similar to pastorals, wherein persons are portrayed as simple country folk although, in reality, they are not. This style was popular in England and France during the 1700s.

Biedermeier Style (1815–1848)

Known mainly as a furniture style in Austria and Germany from about 1800 to 1860. In painting, it was popular in Austria, Germany, Switzerland and Denmark with realism as its essence in the depiction of landscape, genre and still-life. Nature was depicted in almost photographic reality by Negg (1782–1863); Olivier (1785–1841); Richter (1803–1884); Stifter (1805–1868); Gauermann (1807–1862); among others. The new middle class (petit bourgeois) was portrayed in scenes with simplicity and coziness as dominant themes. Waldmuller (1793–1865); Fendi (1796–1842); von Amerling (1803–1887); Danhauser (1805–1845); among others. Genre scenes were painted by Spitzweg (1808–1885); Hasenclever (1810–1853); Heine (1813–1839); Hubner (1814–1879); among others.

Bildarchitektur (Pictorial Architecture)

A term coined by Kassak (1887–1967), an important figure in the Central European avant-garde movement. It was his theory that Bildarchitektur painting was a symbol of action: that non-objective art was to become a political statement without relaying any story. Geometric forms and pure colors, according to Kassak, were signs of truth.

Binder

Any material that holds particles of pigment together.

Biomorphic Abstraction

A form suggesting a living organism, in contrast to geometric or lifeless form.

Bird's-Eye View

A scene depicted as though observed far above it.

Black American Art

Several well-known black American artists:

Johnston a/k/a Johnson (active 1796–1824) A self-taught artist who was the first black American to gain recognition during his own lifetime. He was a portraitist of Baltimore's prosperous merchant and planter families.

Duncanson (1822–1872) His ouevre consisted of romantic landscape, portraits and still-life. He was influenced by the Hudson River School.

Bannister (1828–1901) His standing in New England was high. He depicted harmonious and spiritual landscapes as an expression of his religious beliefs.

Traylor (1855–1947) An illiterate farmer whose period of artistic activity from 1939 to 1942 produced about 1500 drawings. He favored the depiction of domestic animals and is known primarily as a folk artist.

Tanner (1859–1937) He studied with Eakins and was an inspiration to other black American artists during his lifetime. His mileau was genre and landscape and particularly religious themes. His draftsmanship was in the academic tradition.

Pippin (1888–1946) His work is characterized by a decorative but sophisticated, primitive style. He painted historic events, Biblical scenes, and his recollections of childhood and war experiences. He favored still-life. Pippin was known for his graphic work for publications and established himself as a master of color and design. His mural epic "Aspects of Negro Life" (1934) contains a section called "From Slavery through Construction."

Thomas (1891–1978) Her abstract paintings were executed in lavish, vibrant colors. She was inspired by the world around her, especially flowers.

Evans (1892–1987) A folk artist whose vividly, almost psychedelically, colored art was often inspired by dreams and religious visions, with emphasis on floral, human, animal and mythical figuration. She often used whatever materials were on hand: scrap paper, window shades, bookbindings, etc. Her mediums were oil, ink or crayon.

Douglas (1899–1979) He was called the "father" of black art in his role as an exponent of black iconography in contemporary art. He was also regarded as a leader of black consciousness.

Savage (1900–1962) She became the nation's youngest known sculptor, as well as a teacher and a spokesperson for black artists. She preferred to model with clay; her work is considered humorous.

Woodruff (1900–1980) His early murals of black history are best known. In later years, he painted in an abstract style, often incorporating black imagery into his work.

Johnson (1901–1970) He painted images of black life in a flat, naive-like manner. He incorporated the imagery of his heritage and childhood into a primitive art which was recognized as unique in its expression of black culture.

Bearden (1914–1988) His vivid, kaleidoscopic paper collages are imaginative and expressive of the life and experience of the black American, especially as seen in street scenes and in the South.

Lawrence (b. 1917) His figures are painted flatly and he uses a combination of bright colors with blacks and browns, giving the overall effect of symbolism. Lawrence is acknowledged as a pioneer in illustrating the struggle of his people for equal rights and in depicting ghetto life. He painted a series on Coast Guard life during World War II, as well as a series in the 1950s called "Struggle: From the History of the American People" in which history from the days of the Indians to present-day life is portrayed in 60 paintings.

Biggers (b. 1924) He portrays the spiritual beauty of black Americans in fields, farmlands and in nature.

Long (b. 1940) An artist who uses both abstract and representational styles, his philosophy is that artists represent the future and viewers of art should understand what the artist sees. He wants to tune into the lives of the masses.

Williamson (b. 1951) Domestic scenes, including exotic flowers and birds, with emphasis on human figuration, appear as literary efforts to depict dream-like perceptions in her paintings of oil on paper.

Blue Rider, The (der Blaue Reiter) (1911–1914)

Another German Expressionist group with Marc (1880–1916) and Kandinsky (1866–1944) as its exponents. They published the almanac "Der Blaue Reiter" which contained articles on the fine arts, music, theatre, and reproductions of diverse art forms from several countries and from other ages. The group's aim was to demonstrate the qualities of artistic expression and to liberate artists from traditional restrictions. The artists wanted to show what was essential in art when they used visual symbols and unrealistic, expressive color to convey strong emotion. Their primitive-like style was used for the depiction of forms from nature and the beauty of the world, including scenes from urban life. Jawlensky (1864–1941); Feininger (1871–1956); Munter (1877–1962); Klee (1879–1940); Macke (1887–1914); among others. See November Group.

Boards

Various types of stiff papers made from cheap fibre to be used as grounds.

Bohemian School (1350–1390)

Formed by Emperor Charles IV who gathered painters from Germany, France, Italy and Bohemia. The artists were influential in the development of International Gothic.

Bolognese School

L. Carracci (1555–1619); Agnostino Carracci (1557–1602); Annibale Carracci (1560–1609); Mastelletta (1575–1655); Cavedone (1577–1660); Tiarini (1577–1668); Domenichino (1581–1641).

Brandywine Tradition

A photographically realistic style promoted by the illustrator Pyle (1853–1911) in the late 1800s. He taught and influenced many illustrators, including N. C. Wyeth (1882–1945) whose family members and students further advanced this style. A museum has been established in Chadds Ford, Pennsylvania to permanently house the works of the Wyeth family considered by many to be the first family of American art today. See **Illustrator** and the **Peale Family**.

Bravura

A show of technical brilliance.

Brethren, The

A name used by those who belonged to the Pre-Raphaelite Brotherhood.

Bridge, The (die Brucke) (1905–1913)

The first German Expressionist group, formed by Kirchner (1880–1938) in Dresden. Its style was characterized by naivety, deformation, strident colors, coarsening of technique and a primitive-like manner of painting. The artists wanted to capture the essence of reality in form and color. Their themes were social and political messages, landscape, nude portraiture, and religious scenes, all expressive of passion and emotion in an attempt to arrive at the basis of human character. They were influenced from three major sources: African/Oceanic sculpture, medieval German woodcuts and children's art. Woodcuts for the wide dissemination of prints became a popular medium. Although the artists proclaimed a kinship with German art of the 1500s, they considered their work to be "a bridge to the future." Gallen-Kallela (1865–1931); Nolde (1867–1956); Mueller (1874–1930);

Peckstein (1881–1955); Heckel (1883–1970); Schmitt-Rotluff (1884–1976); among others. See The Blue Rider and New Artists Alliance.

Brown Sauce

A pejorative term used to describe the dark glazes of 19th century paintings.

Brushwork

A general term for the style in which paint is applied and is considered an important aspect of the artist's "handwriting." See Signature Style.

Buckeye

A disparaging term for stereotyped, mass-produced landscape pictures.

Byzantine Art (330–1453 A.D.)

The development of art in Constantinople which inherited its civilization from Rome, with the difference, however, that in Byzantium the illusion of reality declined and two-dimensional flatness and stillness took precedence. This period includes the art produced in the Christian world when Western art became Byzantine in style. The more simple art of the Early Christian era was replaced by grandeur. Churches were built everywhere and decorated with mosaics—the chief decoration for 1,000 years in Eastern churches. Decorative sculpture, manuscript illumination, ivory carving, metalwork and enameling were the primary arts and crafts, with pictorial art represented in wall and panel painting—all of which reached their fullest expression in the 6th century in the reign of Justinian. In 726 Emperor Leo III declared that symbols of Christianity, rather than figurative art, were preferable. During this Iconoclastic crisis existing works of art were removed or destroyed. It ended, however, in 843 and the Byzantine style continued. Although the term Byzantine actually embraced a variety of painting styles, emphasis was on color effect, flat forms, decorative highlights, with backgrounds of deep color or gold. See Carolingian Renaissance and Romanesque.

C. (abbreviation for circa)
About, approximately.

Cabinet Picture
Easel painting less than 30 inches in width meant to be viewed at close range. See Easel Picture.

California Figurative Painters—See Bay Area Figuration.

Calligraphy
The art of elegant handwriting: a very important art in the form of brushwork in the Orient. It was a strong influence on several American painters, such as Pollock, Tobey and Tomlin.

Camden Town Group (1911–1913)
An English movement whose artists practiced different styles. Their commonality was the dislike for academic tradition and an inclination toward art of the Post-Impressionists and the representation of everyday scenes. Sickert (1860–1942); L. Pissarro (1863–1944); Bevan (1865–1925); Gilman (1876–1919); Gore (1878–1914); Ginner (1878–1952); among others.

Camera Obscura a/k/a/ Camera Ottica
A mechanical aid sometimes referred to as a "magic box." It was used by Venetian and Dutch landscape artists to trace the visual relationships of size and shape in drawing from nature.

Canvas
1. A prepared cloth surface used in oil painting.
2. A reference to a finished oil painting.

Capriccios
1. A term used for paintings of real or imaginary ruins in charming groupings.
2. Goya (1746–1828) used this term for a series of paintings in which he depicted witches, monsters and other creatures.

Caricature
A comical, satirical or grotesque rendering by means of distortion or exaggeration.

Carolingian Renaissance (786–877)

Under the aegis of Charlemagne and Charles the Bold, the revival of art and literature was made possible through a re-awakened interest in Greek and Roman culture. The great works of antiquity survived because Charlemagne caused them to be copied. Illuminated manuscripts were outstanding. The Utrecht Psalter (804) is classic. Schools of painting were also encouraged. See Illumination and Ottonian Renaissance.

Cartoon

1. A preparatory design, drawing or painting.
2. The drawing of comic strips or cartoons that have a message or story to convey beneath the surface, especially as in political satire.

Cast, Casting

A sculptural process wherein a liquid is poured into a mold and allowed to harden.

Cave Art

The recently discovered Cave Art of Lascaux, France in 1940 and of Altamira, Spain in 1879 are estimated to be about 15,000 years old. Generally, the figures depicted are animals, probably drawn or carved in the hope that the naturalistic representations, which were painted in various ochres, reds and blacks, would exert a certain magic realism so that the animals would succumb to their weapons. Cave Art has also been discovered in other parts of Europe. Other Old Stone Age art was in the form of carvings in bone, horn or stone. Female figures are known as Venuses. Middle Stone Age art was characterized by the painting of geometric designs on small pebbles or rocks. New Stone Age art was characterized by pottery with geometric designs and the erection of huge stones to mark burial grounds.

It is apparent that the creation of form and decoration was almost standard in cultures of corresponding periods of development.

Ceramics

The craft of making sculptures and decorative objects of household use (plates, vases, etc.) from earthenware, porcelain, enamels, etc.

Chance Configuration

Arp (1887–1966) was the first to cut shapes without thought and to arrange them according to chance. Duchamp (1887–1968) dropped threads on a canvas and then traced them.

Chiaroscuro (Clear/Obscure)

The distribution of light and dark and the contrast between them to create an illusion of depth and space. According to Leonardo da Vinci, it is "the true and natural arrangement of light and shade."

Chiaroscuro in Nature

1. The creation of mood in landscape resulting from the play of light and shade.
2. The glow of sunlight on landscape.

Chinese Art

Over a period of 3500 years the art of China has remained quiet and conservative. Central to its theme was the expression of ideas and feelings, along with representations of nature, in contrast to religious themes of other countries in the early stages of their culture.

During the early centuries, the ruling class created tombs of extraordinary size in which paintings and ceramic sculptures by the thousands were installed. Their burial chambers were similar to those of the Egyptians where vivid scenes were depicted.

Painting and calligraphy have been respected as the highest art forms for centuries. Poetry is intimately fused with painting: the poem inspires the artist. The crafts of ivory carving and laquer-work were outstanding. Porcelain objects were highly prized. Bronze casting was known of c. 1700 B.C.

In the 6th century, Six Principles of Painting were formulated by the painter Hsieh Ho. These principles have remained the fundamental rules of technique to the present day. They are, in fact, similar to those formulated by Western academicians.

The calligraphic brushstroke has always been of prime importance. It has been the ambition of artists to acquire such ease with brush and ink so as to write a fresh vision immediately. Basically, paintings are marked by light and sketchy lines because of the materials and techniques used: light brush, wash and black ink. The Chinese feel that repetitive copying enhances personal technique.

Two schools evolved in the 16th and 17th centuries. Painters in the Northern (academic) school became known for decoration and romantic realism; those of the Southern school became known for their grasp of the inner nature of things and high ideals.

After China opened its doors to Western trade, the calligraphic brushstroke was counterbalanced by bold colors, perspective and chiaroscuro. And as the old order of things collapsed, the desire for change and innovation became paramount. China's first art school established in 1912 offered classes in both Western and Chinese style, and figure painting, which had disappeared for almost 1,000 years, made a strong comeback.

Thousands of art treasures were destroyed during the recent Cultural Revolution and it is only lately that, aside from political posters, original art has emerged. The Yunnan school, for example, formulated by Jiang Tie-Fang and fellow artists, expresses the belief that art is based on individual creative vision, not philosophy. The school established itself as a pioneer of contemporary art, but with the ideal of retaining a long view of Chinese art history. See **Oriental Art.**

Christina's World

One of the best known works of art by an American artist in the 20th century. A Wyeth (b. 1917).

Cinquecento

Designating the 500s (1500s) during the Renaissance, an age when Venetian art and architecture reached their peak.

Cityscape

1. A view of a city or a part of it.
2. A term used to describe the ingredients of urban life, such as street signs, cafes, newspapers, etc.

When Kokoschka (1886–1980) toured European cities for seven years, his intention was to paint cosmic views of the cities that were expressive of his own feelings. This series is called "The Painted World."

Sloan (1871–1951), Berthelsen (1883–1969), Marsh (1898–1954), R. Soyer (1899–1987), and Downes (b. 1939), among others, are known for their cityscapes of New York City. See **Ashcan School, 14th Street School, Veduta and View Painting.**

Classic

Referring to quality, not style. Monet's work would be considered classic or a typical example of Impressionism.

Classical Art

Referring to Greek, Roman and Renaissance art. Simplicity, harmony and balance are its underlying features. Most art forms recognized by the modern world can be traced to the Classical world of art. Also, a term used to describe art of lasting quality.

Classical Revival—See Neoclassicism.

Classicism

1. The use of classical models.
2. Allegiance to traditional universal standards.

Clip Art

Camera-ready art that is sold to newspapers and other publications that need small pieces of Graphic Art. Since there is no copyright, the purchaser can change the design. Clip Art is available from low cost books full of designs to high quality work produced on single sheets.

Cloisonnism a/k/a/ Pont-Aven Style

This style evolved from the paintings of Gauguin (1848–1903) and Bernard (1868–1941) who applied paint thinly and bound the unmodeled flat colored areas with bold outlines; the effect of stained glass resulted. This was a step in the direction of Synthetism.

Closed Edition—See Limited Edition.

CoBrA (1948–1951)

A Dutch reactionary movement led by Appel (b. 1921) and made up of experimental artists from Copenhagen, Brussels and Amsterdam who wanted to explore the subconscious and fantastic imagery. Jorn called it "an abstract art that does not believe in abstraction." Strong colors and human figuration were the vehicles of expression; their themes were formulated on Primitive Art, Folk Art and children's art. They had a great impact on Northern Europe. Jorn (1914–1973); Corneille (b. 1922); Alechinsky (b. 1927); among others.

Cold Art

A term referring to the use of mathematics in constructions.

Collage (Mounting/Pasting)

The technique of building up a picture in two-dimensional form or low relief, which emerged from the work of Picasso (1881–1973) and Braque (1882–1963). In essence, nonart materials (newspaper, wallpaper, wood, etc.) were applied to the canvas with drawn or painted sketches made over the principal features of the subject. This technique was considered a turning point in 20th century art. The language of Cubism was worked out through collage. See Cubism.

Collage Painting

An art form peculiar to Marca-Relli (b. 1913) wherein painted cut-outs from canvas are attached to a ground in expressive combinations. Black glue is used to outline the forms. See Femmage.

Color Field Painting (1950s–1960s)

The term Color Field has been used to describe the work of a number of modern artists who used color as both form and content. There is no central focus. The canvas is so large that the viewer's field of vision seems to be engulfed by color that reaches out to infinity. Rothko (1903–1970); Newman (1905–1970); Louis (1912–1962); Olitsky (b. 1922); Noland (b. 1924); among others. See Minimalism.

Combine Painting (1950s)

A term used to describe the large anti-formalist assemblages of Rauschenberg (b. 1925) who incorporated three-dimensional objects with painted canvases or photographic images. Occasionally, the Combines are free-standing.

Commercial Artist

An artist who is employed to work in various fields: advertising, illustration, etc.

Complex Forms

A group of generally unknown but related units.

Composed Objects

Objects are irrationally combined as in Surrealism.

Composition

The arrangement of parts to present a unified picture. Its components are order, balance, harmony and clarity.

Computer Art

Several practical uses of the computer in contemporary art are:

1. As a sketch pad to make as many variations of an image as desired.
2. As a tool to manipulate and analyze the ideas and thoughts of the artist.
3. The writing of programs to construct modes of creative expression.
4. Mathematical calculations of shape and form.
5. Calculations of pigment proportions for color variations.
6. Images produced on the computer screen can be used in photographic reproduction and enlargement.

Computer Portrait Sculpture

A technique of sculpture which is initiated with a three-dimensional digitized image that is taken with a special lighting video camera and a computer set-up. Thereafter, a milling machine that is controlled by the computer cuts out the sculpture; this operation normally requires two or three hours for completion. A sculptor will then sharpen some of the contours after which it is coated with epoxy and a bronze powder to make a proof. It is then sent to a foundry where a mold is made in which bronze is poured. By Cyberware Laboratories, California. See **Holography**.

Conception

1. The capacity of forming or understanding ideas or abstractions.
2. A general idea.

Conceptual Art (1960s–1970s)

Its existence was communicated through ideas, words or images. It was not sited, but occasionally became physical as a Performance Art. The artist wanted the viewer to focus on and understand the concept behind the work rather than the end product. Occasionally, a certificate affirming the right to reproduce the "art" was given to a purchaser. LeWitt (b. 1928), one of its exponents, said: "The idea or the concept is the most important aspect of the work. . . . The idea becomes the machine that makes the art. . . ." Its underlying role, however, was a great sense of liberation. Latham (b. 1921); Huebler (b. 1924); Klein (1928–1962); Baldessari (b. 1932); Harrison (b. 1932); Barry (b. 1936); Haacke (b. 1936); Buren (b. 1938); Weiner (b. 1940); among others. See **Process Art, Performance Art** and **Happenings.**

Concrete Art

A term used for nonfigurative painting without any reference to the object world. In other words, a synonym for nonobjective art. It was a recognized term when van Doesburg (1883–1931) issued a manifesto in 1930 regarding its meaning. He stated that art was universal, that art should be entirely planned before its execution, that the picture should be composed only of planes and colors with simplicity and clarity as principal elements, and that the technique employed should be exact. The term "concrete" was not used again until Arp (1887–1966) described his biomorphic sculptural concretions. See **Human Concretions.** By 1938 Kandinsky (1866–1944) indicated his preference for the term to describe his work—in opposition to the term "abstract." The term was also applicable to Abstract-Creation, and was later used by other European artists in the 1960s and 1970s, too numerous to mention.

Cone of Vision

The field of vision of the viewer of a work of art.

Connoisseurship

A special talent developed from the experience of looking, studying and reading about art.

Constructionism—See **Structurism.**

Constructivism (1920s et seq.)

A revolutionary movement concerned with a concept of sculpture, which was formed by Malevich (1878–1935) and developed by the brothers Pevsner (1886–1962) and Gabo (1890–1977) in Moscow. Pevsner and Gabo published "Realistic Manifesto" in 1920, which proved to be a landmark in art history. They declared that space, movement and time were the essential elements of life; they rejected modelling, volume and mass. (The relief sculptures of Tatlin (1885–1953) were very influential on the origins of Constructivism.) Essentially, it was a functional art, often using factory-made materials, and based on nonobjective, three-dimensional, sculpture-like forms with dynamic and spatial concepts. Constructivism opened the door to various techniques in the plastic arts, especially experimentation with space, light and motion by a number of American artists. Gonzalez (1876–1942); Duchamp (1887–1968); Moholy-Nagy (1895–1946); Lippold (b. 1915); Gussow (b. 1918); DiSuvero (b. 1933); among others. See **Mobile, Kinetic Art and Sculpture** and **Structurism.**

Contemporary Art
It usually reflects the period in which the artist lives—according to the artist's perception or conception. It involves diverse styles, innovative techniques and materials available.

Content
The subject matter or motif of a work combined with certain aesthetic values. Form and content are the two major elements of a work of art.

Continuous Style/Representation
An artistic technique which depicts several continuing episodes in one picture or relief sculpture—a form often used in Roman art. See **Trajan Column.**

Contour
The outline of a shape which is used to express movement, volume or quality.

Contrast
Any strong difference between two or more juxtaposed colors or patterns.

Contropposto (opposed)
Referring to the portrayal of the human body so that the upper portion moves in one direction and the lower portion in another, in an effort to create movement and tension. It was a device commonly used in classical Greek sculpture.

Convention, Conventional
Lacking originality or individuality.

Coptic Art (300–600 A.D.)
Art of the Early Christians in Egypt when Egypt was part of the Roman and Byzantine Empires. Wall paintings were flat and stylized. Arts and crafts were woven tapestries, stone and ivory carvings, manuscript illumination and pottery.

Copy
A copy of a painting may have historical or documentary value. A gallery copy is executed by a professional copyist. A variant is a copy with changes made by the original artist or a copy made by an imitator. A replica is an exact copy done by the original artist or under his direction.

Corporate Art
A relatively new field wherein corporations purchase contemporary art of known and unknown artists, most often with the assistance of consultants. An important reason for the existence of Corporate Art is that it helps create an environment in which it is both enjoyable and profitable to do business. The underlying benefits, however, are that corporations are funding local, regional and national arts organizations as well as donating money and art to museums along with ideas and skills.

Cotex
A Late Roman or Early Christian book which served as a model for the production of religious texts. The practice was to preface the book with a portrayal of the author. The copyist then went on to decorate pages and illustrate the narrative.

Craftsmanship
The use of tools and materials in a skillful manner. Materials commonly used are textiles, clay, metal, wood and glass.

Cryptogram
A drawing, painting or writing with a hidden meaning.

Cubism (1907–1925)
Cezanne (1839–1906), who reacted against Impressionism, is considered the forerunner of Cubism because of his structured style. He was concerned with the cube, the sphere and the cone in his painted "constructions after nature." The Cubist movement was initiated by Picasso (1881–1973) and Braque (1882–1963) who worked together in France to find new expression.

Their discoveries began a new visual language (not a style) that was adapted by many avant-garde artists according to their own interpretation of that language. Two major divisions of Cubism exist:

—Analytical Cubism (breaking apart): The first stage (1907–1912) was a technique that was translated from collage into oil painting. Essentially, it was the presentation of different views of a subject in the same picture. The Cubist put into the picture what the mind knows exists—the other side of the figure or object—resulting in multiple viewpoints, with the parts being broken apart and then re-arranged, making it somewhat difficult to decipher, a sort of incomprehensible mental puzzle. Cubes of monochromatic, muted colors dominated. Gleizes (1881–1953); Leger (1881–1955); Marcoussis (1883–1941); Metzinger (1883–1956); La Fresnaye (1885–1925); Delaunay (1885–1941); Lipchitz (1891–1973); among others. See **Bateau-Lavoir Group.**

—Synthetic Cubism (building up or putting together): The second stage (1912–1914) grew out of a method of plane sculpture created by Picasso—a kind of drawing in space. One of his first attempts was to create a guitar from nonart materials by skillfully arranging two-dimensional form in three-dimensional space. A brighter palette of colors was also introduced. Gris (1887–1927), considered a classic Synthetic Cubist, developed a technique whereby he would plan the structure of his painting and then arrange the flat symbols of dimensionality on the framework. By the 1920s Braque had developed another technique which he continued to practice until his death. See **Puteau Group, Orphism and Vorticism.**

Cubist Realism a/k/a/ Precisionism (1915–1920s)

Clean-edge, geometric forms that were introduced into paintings of plants, machinery, simple architecture, etc. Forms were simplified to the point of abstraction, but remain recognizable. Bluemner (1867–1938); Schamberg (1882–1918); Demuth (1883–1935); Spencer (1883–1952); Sheeler (1883–1965); O'Keefe (1887–1986); Cross (1901–1973); Crawford (1906–1975); among others.

Cubist Sculpture

During the Synthetic stage of Cubism, a number of sculptors adapted its principles to sculpture. Duchamp-Villon (1876–

1918); Gonzalez (1876–1942); Laurens (1885–1954); Archipenko (1887–1964); Lipchitz (1891–1973); among others.

Cubo-Futurism

Rather than an art movement, it was more a theory expounded in 1912/1913 by the Russian poet Kruchenykh who quoted, "Art goes in the vanguard of psychic evolution." It represented art of the transcendent, something outside ordinary human experience, in the hope that the consciousness would be altered to a state similar to that achieved through Yoga discipline. Its adherents believed that everything in the universe possessed an inner being—that nothing was inanimate. Matiushin (1861–1931); Malevich (1878–1935); B. Ender (1893–1960); Kudriashev (1896–1970); M. Ender (1897–1942); among others. See Rayonism, Suprematism and Zaum.

Curator

One who selects the art, supervises its installation and takes care of a place of exhibition.

Currier & Ives (1835–1907)

A printmaker who mass-produced lithographic prints depicting American life. In all, about 7,000 scenes were produced. One of the best known was "Home for Thanksgiving" by Durrie (1820–1862). Currier & Ives prints provided a guide to American culture and taste of the 1800s.

Cycle Series

Paintings linked by theme, a style often used in fresco painting.

Dada (1916–1922)

A rebellion against modern development which grew on an international scale. Basically, it expressed itself in words. Art, in its secondary role, played a constructive part. Essentially, Dada was anarchic and nihilistic in its attempt to get rid of the dead weight of social and artistic traditions, affirming that nothing more was to be said. Its intention was to cleanse and revive art and to liberate visual conception with found objects, ready-mades, collages and assemblages. Schwitters (1877–1948); Picabia (1879–1953); Delaunay (1885–1941); Arp (1887–1966); Duchamp (1887–1968); Ernst (1891–1976); among others. See Surrealism.

Danube School

Referring to those artists located near the Danube in the 1500s, who used lush landscape and rich color as a vital part of their representations of nature and drama. Cranach (1472–1553); Altdorfer (1480–1538); Huber (1490–1553); among others.

Darkening

A phenomenon that occurs in oil painting because of undesirable factors.

Death Mask

A plaster cast molded on the face of a deceased person, a practice popular in Roman times.

Decalcomania

A technique developed by Surreal artists, most notably Dominquez (1901–1956) who placed a newly painted surface against a second surface. In the process a spontaneous blurred effect was created. The images of animals, wheels and rocks are considered his best works. Ernst (1891–1976) pressed two newly painted canvases together and then pulled them apart. He used the resulting patterns as starting points for new paintings. See Frottage and Grattage.

Decomposition

To undergo a breakdown.

Decorative

Aesthetically pleasing; non-functional.

Decorative Arts

Synonymous with Applied art, sometimes called "minor arts."

Degenerate Art

The exhibition of Modern Art by the Nazis when they confiscated the work of many well known artists. In reality, the paintings were auctioned off for the financial benefit of the Nazi party. The artists themselves were either banned, exiled or imprisoned.

Delineate

To portray or to describe in sharp, vivid detail.

Depouiller

A word used by Miro, meaning to strip, to render bare, to eliminate all unnecessary flourish.

Derivative

Referring to material appropriated or borrowed from the work of other artists.

Desacralization

The travesty of sacred-like art subjects, such as the Mona Lisa with a beard and a mustache.

Design

1. An arrangement of colors, lines, forms or textures.
2. A decorative pattern.
3. The overall scheme.

DeStijl—Look under S.

Detail

A small or minute part of a work of art.

Detonography

An artistic medium peculiar to E. Rosenberg (b. 1942) whereby she molds plaster onto a panel, occasionally adding found objects or impressions. Thereafter, the mold is taken to a blasting range where it is covered with a sheet of metal and plastic explosive. After explosion, a perfect replica of the mold has been transferred to the metal sheet. The result is a bas relief executed in fine detail.

Deutscher Werkbund

A progressive German association of manufacturers, architects, artists and writers formed in 1907 to promote quality in the production of art and architecture. It had a widespread influence on other European countries.

DIAS (Destruction in Art Symposium) (1960s)

A Dada-like movement formed in England and the U.S. to participate in activities such as "Destruction Happenings" and "Destruction Events." Tinguely (b. 1925); Metzger (b. 1926); Haacke (b. 1936); among others.

Dimension

A measure in one direction.

Diorama

A three-dimensional scene with a painted background.

Diptych

1. A painting or altarpiece consisting of two parts.
2. A work made of two matching parts.

Distortion

A lack of proportionality. In Modern Art, a deviation from convention in the rendition of color, form or perspective.

Divisionism—See Neo-Impressionism.

Docent

A person who is an extension of the educational department of a museum and conducts guided tours.

Draftsperson

One who is skilled in the basics of drawing or sketching.

Drawing

1. The definition of shape and form by line in various ways.
2. The reproduction of a subject in line with a studied approach.

Its various mediums include charcoal, ink, pencil, chalk, metal point and crayon. (Sketching is done spontaneously in a short period of time representing a more casual approach.) Ingres' dictum: "Drawing is the integrity of art."

Drawing in Space

A term ascribed to the sculptural work of Lassaw (b. 1913) who bent, welded and soldered wire into strong, organic form. His first abstract work in 1931 made him a pioneer of abstract sculpture in the U.S. He was influential on the work of Lipton (1903–1986); Ferber (b. 1906) and Roszak (1907–1981). The work of D. Smith (1906–1965) in forged metal can also aptly be described as "drawing in space."

Drip Painting

The technique of applying paint by dripping, pouring, etc. onto canvas. The artists well known for this method are Hofmann (1880–1966); Pollock (1912–1956) and Francis (b. 1923). See **Action Painting.**

Duco Paint

The use of automobile enamel by some modern-day artists.

Dummy Board Figures

Life-size cut-outs of human figures are placed in genre and domestic scenes, to be painted in oils.

Dutch School

A. Bloemaert (1564–1651); Hals (1580–1666); van Honthorst (1590–1656); Claesz (1594–1680); van Campen (1595–1657); van Goyen (1596–1656); Jansz (1597–1665); H. Bloemaert (1601–1672); Rembrandt (1606–1669); Dou (1613–1675); Both (1615–1652); Ter Borch (1617–1681); deWitte (1617–1692); Kalf (1619–1693); van Beyeren (1620–1690); Cuyp (1620–1691); Fabritius (1622–1654); Steen (1626–1679); van Aelst (1626–1683); van Ruisdael (1628–1682); Metsu (1629–1667); de Hooch (1629–1677); Vermeer (1632–1675); van der Heyden (1637–1712); Hobbema (1638–1709); van de Velde (1642–1679); van de Cappelle (1642–1679).

Early Christian Art (200s–300s)

The Early Christians rejected the classical tradition because of new religious ideals, and in so doing changed the purpose and character of art. Because of a belief in resurrection, the Early Christians continued the Roman practice of burying the dead in catacombs which were painted in earthen colors and decorated with illusionistic representations. These are the best known paintings. During the age of persecution, artists used a code of symbols: the fish for Christ, a loaf for Holy Communion, etc. There was little wealth among the Early Christians which resulted in the creation of a simple but fine art in the form of wall frescoes. After Christianity was accepted, art took the form of narrative relief to illustrate Biblical themes. See **Byzantine Art.**

Early Renaissance (the 1400s: Quattrocento)

Florence, as the new Athens, was hailed as the champion of freedom as well as the home of arts and crafts. As such, it offered opportunities for diverse creative talents. Art was reclassified as a liberal art. In this new place of high esteem, the artist was looked upon as a person of learning and culture. Donatello (1386–1466), a sculptor, and Brunelleschi (1377–1446), an architect, as well as Alberti (1404–1472), an architect and a writer who established the principles of naturalism through perspective and the dramatic composition of figures, were considered founding fathers of the Renaissance. Perspective, outline and knowledge of the body became characteristic of Italianate painting. Masaccio (1401–1428) and Uccello (1397–1475) were among the first painters to master the illusion of three dimensionality through aerial perspective and linear perspective, respectively. See **High Renaissance.**

Earth Art a/k/a/ Land Art or Earthworks (1960s–1970s)

A view of natural inland scenery involving the rearrangement, shifting, cutting, etc. of portions of the earth, enabling the spectator to view the landscape as a "presence" with abstract suggestions. It also constituted an interest in ecology and a nostalgia for ruins. Some of the works, however, were destructive. Morris (b. 1931); DeMaria (b. 1935); Andre (b. 1935); Haacke (b. 1936); Smithson (1938–1973); D. Oppenheim (b. 1938); among others.

Easel

An adjustable stand to support a canvas or board during the creation of a painting or for display of the finished product.

Easel Picture

A movable framed painting developed during the Renaissance specifically to be displayed on easels. See **Cabinet Picture.**

Eclecticism

1. The practice of appropriating and combining the best features from various styles and techniques in the hope of producing a new style.
2. The absence of a personal style by the artist.

Eggbeater Series (1927–1928)

A series of abstract paintings whereby Davis (1894–1964) attempted to rid himself of any illusion when he repeatedly painted an eggbeater, an electric fan and a rubber glove until they ceased to exist except as color, line and shape. He also produced a series of cityscapes of Paris (1928–1929). Davis called his works "color-space compositions."

Egyptian Art (3200–332 B.C.)

Egyptian art was uncommonly self-contained. Its art forms were usually related to architecture (pyramids, temples, obelisks, etc.) and sculpture executed in high relief. Genre paintings on pottery and other useful objects were marked by strong line, regular patterns, harmony, lack of emotion, flatness, descriptive perspective and a multitude of colors.

Aristocratic Egyptians were concerned with the happy afterlife and preservation of the body. They saw art as the keynote in service to the gods. Tombs were heavily decorated with painted reliefs narrating the lives of decedents. Statues were placed at the doors of tombs. As the years passed, metalwork and sculpture became quite advanced. Egyptian achievements were influential on Greek and Roman art.

The Eight

Referring to a group of artists and their associates who exhibited together in 1908. Essentially, their theme was urban realism. The exhibition proved to be one of the milestones in Modern Art in that the public evinced an interest in new movements. The group changed the face of American art. (Several members were referred to as the Ashcan School.) Prendergast (1859–1924); Davies (1862–1928); Henri (1865–1929); Luks (1867–1933); Glackens (1870–1938); Sloan (1871–1951); Lawson (1873–1939); Shinn (1876–1953); Bellows (1882–1925); among others. See **Ashcan School** and **American Scene Painting.**

El Paso (1957–1960)
A group of artists who wanted to establish Spain as a creative center and to encourage other painters of Expressive Abstraction. Their revolutionary object was "the free unfolding of art and the artist." Millares (1926–1972); M. Rivera (b. 1927); Saura (b. 1930); Canogar (b. 1934). See **Art Informel.**

Embellish
To beautify with ornamentation.

Embossing
The raised design on a surface such as paper, silver, etc.

Enamel
Colorless, white or colored glass fused by heat to a metal or porcelain base to produce a smooth, glossy appearance. Also, the object so produced.

Encaustic Wax Paint
A pigment tempered with hot liquid wax that is painted on canvas while it is still hot.

Engaged
A sculpture that is not free standing; rather, it is attached to another element.

English School
Hilliard (1547–1619); Mutens (1590–1642); van Dyck (1599–1641); Cooper (1609–1672); Riley (1646–1691); Dahl (1656–1743); Hogarth (1697–1764); Hayman (1708–1776); Ramsay (1713–1784); Wilson (1714–1782); Reynolds (1723–1792); Stubbs (1724–1806); Sandby (1725–1809); Gainsborough (1727–1788); Barrett (1732–1784); Romney (1734–1802); Towne (1739–1816); Cozens (1752–1799); Raeburn (1756–1823); Crome (1768–1821); Lawrence (1769–1830); Girtin (1775–1802); Turner (1775–1851); Constable (1776–1837); Callcott (1779–1844); Cotman (1782–1842); Cox (1783–1859); Frith (1819–1909).

Environments/Assemblages (1950s–1960s)
The combination of the qualities of painting, sculpture, collage, theatre and spectator participation. Beuys (1921–1986); Segal (b. 1924); Morris (b. 1931); Grooms (b. 1937); among others. See Sculpto-Pictoramas.

Equestrian Portrait
A portrait usually of a great personage seated on a horse.

Eskimo Art—See North American Indian and Eskimo Art.

Esthetics—See Aesthetics.

Ethnographic Art
The art inspired by a racial culture and especially referring to Primitive Art.

Etruscan Art (600s–400s B.C.)
Before Roman growth, the Etruscans were an important nation in Western Italy. Their artistic expression was reflected in large and small bronze or terracotta sculptures, portrait busts and vase painting. In pictorial art, artists favored reality and the world of nature. Mural work was located in elaborate tombs. Architecture and town-planning were extraordinary. Minor arts consisted of work in ivory and gold and other metalwork. When the Romans displaced the Etruscans, the Greek background of Etruscan art carried over.

Euston Road Group (1930s)
Referring to several English painters who turned to simplicity and a naturalistic, representational style in the rendition of genre, landscapes, portraits, nudes and still-lifes. They opened a school in 1937. Bell (1907–1943); Rogers (1907–1979); Coldstream (b. 1908); Passmore (b. 1908); among others.

Expressionism (1890s–early 1900s)
A subjective style: the artist expressed his moods and feelings with strong colors, bold strokes, movement and distortion. (The word "Expressionism" can be used in any art which distorts reality because of the artist's perception and inner feelings or his expression of the angst of the times.) Figural imagery was a vital element and color was used as an independent force because artists thought of it as symbolic or as creating movement. Al-

though Matisse and the Fauvists are credited with its innovation in modern times, it was essentially a German/Scandinavian movement. El Greco (1541–1614) might be called the first Expressionist, but in Modern Art van Gogh (1853–1890) can be referred to as the "father" of Expressionism because of his style and his subjective feelings about the painted object. Munch (1863–1944) was its most dominant influence in Northern Europe. See Fauvism and German Expressionism.

Expressionist Realism (1914–1930s)

An important style in France wherein participating artists expressed a natural spontaneity in the rendition of nudes, still-lifes, landscapes, etc. First generation artists were Bouche (1874–1941); Defresne (1876–1938); Hervieu (1878–1954); Asselin (1882–1947); L. Moreau (1882–1948); among others. Second generation artists were Aujame (1905–1965); Brayer (b. 1907); Despierre (b. 1912); among others.

Eye-Level or Eye-Line

The subject or scene is painted at eye-level to give a more realistic or natural effect.

Factura (early 1900s)

Cubism as developed in Russia whereby multiple planes and the breaking up of objects were the techniques used in creating collages. It was a strong influence on Constructivism.

Faiyum Portraits

For the first 400 years of the Christian era in Faiyum, Egypt, which was settled by the Greeks, a number of realistically painted portraits were created on wooden panels.

Fantasy

An inventive image or design as perceived in a daydream or a thought.

Far Distance a/k/a/ Offskip

A scene or representation which appears farthest from the eye of the viewer.

Fauvism (1905–1908)

The style of a loosely-formed group of artists in France called "les Fauves" (the Wild Beasts) who promoted no doctrine. Fauvism was characterized by thick line, energy and distortion; pure, vibrant but dissonant color applied with regular brushstrokes; lack of perspective; primitive, universal emotionalism. Color was used broadly with a great sense of liberation. African sculpture played an influence in the formation of their concept of art. Matisse (1869–1954), their informal leader, said, "What I look for above all is expression." Roualt (1871–1958); Levy (1875–1944); Marquet (1875–1947); de Vlaminck (1876–1958); Puy (1876–1960); van Dongen (1877–1968); Derain (1880–1954); among others. See Expressionism.

Federal Art Project (1935–1943)

This project was created during the Great Depression for the purpose of founding local art schools and centers and to provide employment for artists and craftspersons who were encouraged to remain in their communities. No discrimination was made between abstract and representational artists. The statistics are that over 5,000 artists and sculptors were employed, who produced over 160,000 paintings, sculptures, murals and prints. Many of the artists who worked for this project are well known today.

Femmage

A term coined by Schapiro (b. 1924) to describe her colorful work in which elements of collage consisting of pieces of feminine material (lace, chintz, gingham) are combined with Abstract Art.

Field

The flat space or plane defined by its edges within which the artist works.

Figuration

1. The depiction of shapes or recognizable imagery which need not be representational or realistic.
2. Refers to human/animal figures, including the implication of figures.

Filagree

Decorative metalwork that resembles open lacework.

Fine Arts

1. Essentially, those arts which can be enjoyed for their own sake: painting, drawing, sculpture and architecture, including some minor arts.
2. Referring to the creation of beautiful objects.

Flat

Essentially, a two-dimensional picture plane lacking the illusion of perspective. In Modern Art, instead of using perspective, objects are spaced and diminish in size according to distance. The background seems to move forward.

Flecked

Spotted or marked.

Flemish School

Master of Flemalle a/k/a/ Rob. Campin (1378–1444); Limbourg Brothers (active 1399–1439); Hubert van Eyck (d. 1426); Jan van Eyck (1385–1441); van der Weyden (1400–1464); Christus (1410–1472); Bouts (1415–1475); Memling (1430–1494); van der Goes (1444–1482); Bosch (1450–1516); David (1450–1523); A. Bening (d. 1519); Massys (1466–1530); Grossaert (1478–1533); S. Bening (1483–1561); Patinir (1485–1525); van Orley

(1488–1543); van Sorel (1495–1562); Brueghel (1525–1569); Rubens (1577–1640). See Dutch School.

Florentine School

Cimabue (1240–1302); Cavallini (1250–1330); Giotto (1266–1336); Bicci (1373–1452); Fra Angelico (1387–1455); del Castagno (1390–1457); Lorenzo (1392–1411); Uccello (1397–1475); DiGiusto (1400–1450); Venziano (1400–1451); Masaccio (1401–1428); Fra Lippi (1406–1469); Pollaiuolo (1429–1498); Messina (1430–1479); Verrocchio (1435–1488); Signorelli (1441–1523); Botticelli (1444–1510); Dom. Ghirlandaio (1449–1494); Leonardo da Vinci (1452–1519); Dav. Ghirlandaio (1452–1525); Fil. Lippi (1457–1504); B. Ghirlandaio (1458–1497); DiCredi (1458–1537); DiCosimo (1462–1521); Fra Bartolommeo (1475–1517); Michelangelo (1475–1564); Dell Sarto (1486–1531).

Fluxus (1959–1970)

An international movement that played an important role in the history of art in the SoHo area of New York City. It was considered the most dramatic movement of the 1960s in its various formats: concerts, Happenings, publications, street events, games, films, etc. It was a fleeting movement that was recorded in a printed looseleaf book.

Folk Art a/k/a/ Peasant Art

A style portraying the lives of the common people of a certain region. It generally covers three areas:

1. Decorative crafts pertaining to a distinct cultural group.
2. Painting or sculpture produced for practical reasons, such as signs or weathervanes.
3. Painting or sculpture by naive or self-taught artists.

See Naive Art.

Follower of

Similar style; also "style of."

Forces Nouvelles (1930s)

An association of painters in Paris whose ambition was to create new expressive naturalism relating to modern life. Its chief characteristic was academic draftsmanship. Humblot (1907–1962); Despierre (b. 1912); Rohner (b. 1913); among others.

Foreground

A scene or representation which appears closest to the viewer.

Form

1. A three-sided effect created through structural drawing or perspective.
2. The arrangement of parts of a picture or sculpture.
3. To give form or shape to.
4. Descriptive terms, such as basic, complex, expressive, free, functional, geometric, etc., may be applied.

Form and content are the basic elements of art.

Format

1. Any style or arrangement which may be repetitive.
2. An arrangement which is the accepted structure.

Found Object (Objet Trouve)

1. Natural objects, such as driftwood or seashells which are found by chance, to be embodied with collage or sculpture.
2. A beautiful and unique artifact that is displayed as a work of art.

14th Street School

A group of New York City artists who depicted shoppers, office workers, the subway, the street, etc. in an attempt to create a meaningful urban art. They can be considered the "second generation" of the Ashcan School. du Bois (1884–1958); Coleman (1887–1932); Marsh (1898–1954); R. Soyer (1899–1987); Bishop (1902–1988); among others.

Free Form

1. Not restricted to conventional forms.
2. Any curvilinear, asymmetrical shape not bound by hard edges.

Free Standing

Standing alone or on its own foundation without a background.

French School

Clouet (1486–1540); Cousin (1490–1560); DeLyon (1500–1574); L. LeNain (1593–1648); G. la Tour (1593–1652); Vignon

(1593–1670); Poussin (1594–1665); Claude Lorrain (1600–1682); M. LeNain (1607–1677); Largilliere (1654–1746); Watteau (1684–1721); Chardin (1699–1779); Fragonard (1732–1806); David (1748–1825); Lebrun (1755–1842); Michel (1763–1843); Ingres (1780–1867); Corot (1796–1875); Delacroix (1798–1863); Daumier (1808–1879); T. Rousseau (1812–1867); Courbet (1819–1877). See Paris, School of.

Fresco Painting (buon fresco)

An ancient technique for the painting of walls or ceilings to make a lasting picture. Pigments are crushed in water and applied to wet plaster on the wall. It was a popular medium in Italy during the Middle Ages and the Renaissance.

Frieze

A sculptured or ornamental band between a wall paneling and ceiling.

Frottage

The placing of paper or canvas on a textured surface and then rubbing the paper or canvas with a crayon, pencil or a paint-coated roller to get an impression. Ernst (1891–1976) used this technique when he created a series called "Natural History." See Grattage.

Fumage

A technique of Automatism: the moving of a candle flame over a sheet of paper whereby the drops would form into dream-like shapes. It was first used by Paalen (1907–1959).

Function

Designed to serve a certain purpose.

Functionalism

The belief that form should be based on function, especially in the decorative arts and in architecture, but in the hope of producing something possessing beauty.

Funk Art a/k/a/ Sick Art (late 1950s–1960s)

A California group of artists who combined the techniques of Dada and Pop Art in the depiction of the macabre. Essentially, a style combining painting and sculpture, wherein images are presented with emphasis on the bizarre. Paris (b. 1925); Kienholz

(b. 1927); deForest (b. 1930); Conner (b. 1933); Thek (b. 1933); Allan (b. 1936); Wiley (b. 1937); Hudson (b. 1938); among others.

Futurism (1909–1914)

A symbolic, noisy, quasi-political concept, rather than a movement, initiated by the Italian poet F. Marinetti with his manifesto declaring the end of art of the past and the birth of art of the future, an impulse that was adopted by poets, musicians and politicians as well. They rejected all forms of realism or naturalism and believed that all things change rapidly. Motion was their motif. They wanted to go forward into the new world of technology and were inspired by experiments in still photography. It was Marinetti's intention that all human behavior should be seen as art, thereby planting the seed for Happenings or Performance Art. Balla (1871–1958); Carra (1881–1966); Boccioni (1882–1916), its theorist; Severini (1883–1966); Russolo (1885–1947); DeChirico (1888–1978); Bragaglia (1890–1960); among others. See Metaphysical School.

Gallery Copy—See **Copy**.

Genre (kind, type)

The depiction of actual, not ideal, scenes from ordinary life, recording everyman's history. Genre painters paint what they see. Their paintings are usually characteristic of a certain time, place or other condition.

Geometric Abstraction

A style that combines geometric forms with balanced color to achieve harmony. Kupka (1871–1957) and Malevich (1878–1935) are recognized as the first painters of Geometric Abstraction. Its most common approaches are nonobjectivity and reference to something with a supernatural or religious meaning. Malevich's "Suprematist Elements: Two Squares" (1913) may be one of the first severe representations of this style. See **Suprematism, Orphism, DeStijl, Hard-Edge Painting, Post-Painterly Abstraction** and **Purism.**

Geometric Form

Relating to simple forms, such as the circle, square, ovoid, etc. They have been used frequently as allegorical symbols to allude to the mysteries of life.

Geometric Style

1. An art based on geometric forms.
2. A primitive style used by ancient Greeks whereby they portrayed severely stylized animals and figures in vase painting.

German Expressionism

An extension of Fauvism in that the artists used dissonant, aggressive color and primitivism to express themselves. They adopted a jagged brushstroke. By 1913 Expressionism was widespread in Germany and was considered a German art form. See **The Bridge, New Artists Alliance** and **The Blue Rider.**

German School

Witz (1400–1445); Lochner (1400–1451); Schongauer (1430–1491); Pacher (1435–1498); Durer (1471–1528); Cranach (1472–1553); Burgkmair (1473–1531); Grunewald (1475–1528); Breu (1475–1537); Altdorfer (1480–1538); Deutsch (1484–1530);

Baldung-Grien (1484–1545); Huber (1490–1553); Bruyn (1493–1555); Holbein (1495–1543); Beham (1500–1550).

Gesso
A fine plaster often used to prime a canvas so that the surface is ready to be painted.

Giotteschi
A term given to describe the followers, pupils and associates of Giotto (1266–1336).

Giverny Group, The
A group of American painters who were strongly influenced by Monet and lived temporarily near his home/studio in France where American Impressionism was born. Robinson (1852–1896); Rose (1867–1925); Parker (1868–1954); Frieseke (1874–1939); Miller (1875–1943); among others.

Glass Painting
A medium of painting on colorless glass with the production seen on the reverse side. This technique was known of in Europe from centuries past. Those created in the tradition of American Folk Art have proved popular.

Glazing
A thin film of translucent color.

Golden Age of Athens—See Greek Art.

Golden Age of Dutch Painting (1600s)
An age during the Baroque period that was witness to the emergence of many great artists. See **Dutch School.**

Golden Age of English Art
An age in the 1700s which produced a number of fine artists, most notably Gainsborough, Constable, Turner, Reynolds, among others. See **English School.**

Golden Age of Spain (1580–1680)
A time when Spain's empire included parts of Europe, the Americas and the Far East. Under the encouragement of Spanish monarchs and through its European connections, the golden

age in the arts began. Writing, theatre and the fine arts were basically extensions of the religious ideals and mystical nature of the Spanish people.

Golden Painting—See Translucid Painting.

Golden Section

A classical formula used to establish the relationship of parts to the whole.

Goldleaf

Gold that has been thinly beaten and applied as gilding.

Goldsmith

An artisan who makes articles of gold.

Gothic (1150–1400)

Because its birthplace was in France, its original name was Frankish or French. Gothic refers more to the architectural and sculptural arts rather than to painting. In its sculptural form, the Church's beliefs and doctrines were illustrated. Early Gothic pictorial arts were represented by abstract and iconographical "painting with glass" (stained glass), panel painting, frescoes and manuscript illumination.

The 13th century is known as the Age of Great Cathedrals, especially in France. Chartres Cathedral is probably the finest example: its sculpture and stained glass represent the summation of Christian history. Small sculptures made from ivory and other materials were outstanding. Continuity between the Old and New Testaments was manifested by allegory and symbolism, as well as by realism.

During the late 1200s/early 1300s (Dugento and Trecento), aspects of the modern world began to manifest themselves in the work of Cimabue (1240–1302) and Cavallini (1250–1330). With the aid of Byzantine theories, based on Hellenistic discoveries, it was Giotto (1266–1336) of the Florentine school who opened a new world by transcribing Gothic sculpture into painting with the discovery of illusion. He was the first to connect dramatic events with living persons and the first to give movement and to express facial emotion. At the same time, Duccio (1260–1319) of the Sienese school was successful in revitalizing Byzantine art with his mastery of Hellenistic/Roman illusion. He was among the first to create paintings based on nature. Both Giotto and

Duccio had numerous followers. The work of A. Lorenzetti (active 1319–1348) in a series called "The Effect of Good Government in the Country" is evidence of a humanist trend.

The term "Late Gothic" is ascribed to artists in Northern Europe who were the counterpart of the Early Renaissance, most notably the Master of Flemalle (1378–1444), one of the first painters to use oil, and Jan van Eyck (1385–1441) and his brother Hubert (d. 1426) who perfected the technique of oil painting. The brothers van Eyck probably produced the greatest masterpiece of Flemish painting with "The Ghent Altarpiece." Other Flemish painters of the Gothic period were Bouts, Christus, David, Memling, van der Goes. See **Flemish School.**

In Germany, sculpture forged ahead in an expressive and realistic manner. The Master of Naumberg (13th century) and Sluter (1380–1406) achieved a degree of realism never before attained in sculpture. German painters of the Gothic period were von Minden, Lochner, Witz, Schongauer. See **German School.**

In England, Gothic was represented by royal tombs and by statues placed on wall niches in cathedrals.

See **International Gothic, Renaissance** and **North European Art.**

Gouache

A watercolor mixed with white to obtain an opaque effect. Also, a work of art so produced.

Graffito

The decoration of buildings during the Renaissance. In modern days, the term Graffiti is used to describe uninvited drawings and scribblings sprayed on buildings and public transportation by vandals. There has developed a style, however, which imitates Graffiti, but is painted or sprayed on canvas or on commissioned spaces. Haring (b. 1958); Scharf (b. 1958); Basquiat (1960–1988); Greenblatt (b. 1960); among others.

Grand Manner

A term referring to the representation of the human figure in a grand setting, as advocated by academies of art, in emulation of High Renaissance style.

Graphic Arts

Essentially, the arts of drawing and printmaking. Various media are used and, in its broadest sense, it can apply to anything that is linear; specifically, it refers to various print processes.

The earliest woodcut (relief print) was developed in China. By the 1400s, when paper was manufactured and printing was introduced, the woodcut was established in Europe. Next in appearance were playing cards and block-books. Many technical problems were overcome by the skills of Altdorfer, Durer and Schongauer of the German school. Rembrandt is credited with introducing the modern view that Graphic Art can be used as a means of artistic expression. In Modern Art, the Japanese color woodcut was a strong influence on French Impressionism in the 19th century.

Some forms of Graphic Art, such as drawing, engraving, etching and lithography, are classified as fine arts, while other processes, such as typography and printing, have a functional quality.

Well known types of Graphic Art are:

A. Intaglio (cutting below the surface): Wood engraving, etching, drypoint, metal engraving.

B. Relief print (uneven surface): Woodcut, mezzotint, aquatint, drypoint, photoengraving, linocut.

C. Planograph (surface): Lithography (offset or by hand), monotype or decalcomania, silkscreen or serigraph, photographic methods, stencil or pochoir.

This listing is not exclusive. Modern usage of the Graphic Arts continues to develop.

Grattage

A Surreal technique developed by Esteban (b. 1914) in 1938 for the creation of landscapes with plant-like forms, which involved the application of paint with a razor blade. Also, a process similar to Frottage when Ernst (1891–1976) worked in oil to create new forms and textures by scraping newly-painted canvases.

Greek Art

The Greeks made no real distinction between arts and crafts. Its known historical periods include:

1. Protogeometric (1000–900 B.C.)

The Mycenaean influence of arcs and circles is seen on vases; the Greek style, however, is superior and the painted decoration more skillful. The black gloss paint from Bronze Age vases is seen as one of the characteristics of Greek vase art.

2. Geometric (900–725 B.C.)

The decoration of vases and small-scale sculpture had by now developed new patterns alongside older ones. The most common designs were meanders, zigzags and triangles. These abstractions, together with human and animal figuration, were all done within a geometric framework.

3. Archaic (725–480 B.C.)

Eastern (Oriental) forms and techniques were adopted and soon mastered by the Greeks. In form and substance, the Eastern influence consisted of work in the mediums of bronze and ivory in the creation of small sculptures. The biggest influence was that of vase painting; floral devices and new outline drawing (black figures with incised details) were the motifs. It was a vital period and vase painters were held in high esteem: they were called "Little Masters." The Egyptian influence is seen in stone statuary and architecture which were always in close association. A unity of scale developed. Shallow relief was used on gravestones to depict scenes or portraits. Red-figure vase painting in detail became the popular art form.

4. Classical a/k/a/ The Golden Age of Athens (480–323 B.C.)

This period reflected the highest point of Greek ideals and established the tenets of Classical art. One of its manifestations was a great sense of proportion. Sculpture in white marble for the most part was in the round; it was also commonly used in relief for the ornamentation of friezes. A major step forward was the discovery of the technique of bronze-casting which became the favored material for sculpture.(The Chinese had invented bronze-casting in or about 1700 B.C.) Portraiture was important; mosaics, mural and panel painting are known through literature to have been popular. The minor crafts of making coins, jewelry, weapons, utensils were important, but vase painting remained the major form of artistic expression.

5. Hellenistic (323–31 B.C.)

After the death of Alexander, a change occurred. Stone and bronze statuary commemorated events and honored personifications, deities and members of royal families. There was a greater closeness to everyday events, and naturalism, rather than idealism, prevailed. Jewelry and artifacts became finer and more decorative; vase painting declined. In architecture, the Parthenon probably possessed the most perfect exterior that the world had ever seen: its sculpture demonstrated the fullest expression of Greek ideals with human figuration represented in its prime.

The Greeks used their own eyes and experimented in the creation of art to render natural forms through shading, expression and movement; the Egyptians used only their knowledge of art. Myron, in his execution of the sculpture "Discus Thrower" (c. 450 B.C.), is credited with conquering movement; other Greeks were able to master space. Although artists were still looked upon as craftspersons, between 520–420 B.C. an interest in art for its own sake developed and comparisons were made between various schools of art. See **Etruscan Art** and **Roman (Empire) Art.**

Grid

1. Equally spaced horizontal and vertical lines.
2. Lines that are applied in rigid patterns to the canvas.

Grisaille

A monochromatic painting executed in gray shades that appears sculptural—a popular technique in medieval painting.

Ground

1. A support that has been prepared with a thin layer of color, gesso, oil or paste, etc.
2. A surface to which paint is applied.
3. In sculpture, the surface from which a figure projects.

Group Courbet

A group of artists in Barcelona in the early 1900s, including Miro (1893–1984) who painted every detail visible to the eye. Miro's early realistic paintings portrayed a world overflowing with living forms.

Growth Through

Referring to the visibility of underpainting in old pictures because of the loss of pigmentation.

Guerrilla Girls (1980s)

An anonymous group of artists in New York City masquerading in gorilla masks. Their aim is to protest the seemingly sexist attitude of art dealers and curators who underrepresent women artists. Their modus operandi is to plaster posters in public places during midnight "raids," which contain the names of those they accuse of perpetuating discrimination against women artists.

Guild a/k/a company or trade union

A Middle Ages association formed to protect craftsmen, traders and artists. Artists were compelled to join, to obey regulations and to maintain high standards. Gradually, master artists broke away and created their own associations which evolved into academies of art.

Half-Tone Process
An invention in 1878 which made possible the reproduction of monochromatic photographs, paintings or drawings used for newspapers, journals, art books, etc. It meant the end of employment for large art staffs on such publications.

Hand of the Artist
Referring to the artist's brushwork as evidence of the artist's hand and mark of personal identity. See **Brushwork** and **Signature Style.**

Happenings (1960s–1970s)
A term associated with New York City artists whereby the elements of theatre were loosely combined with other art forms: an impromptu Performance Art with plotless theatrical events. Things were made to happen—a kind of "sculpture in action" with audience participation. Kaprow (b. 1937) is believed to have been its original pioneer when he formulated a series called "13 Happenings in 6 Parts" in 1959. In time, Oldenburg (b. 1929), Whitman (b. 1935), Dine (b. 1935) and Grooms (b. 1937) formed a loose group and collaborated in public events, among many others. See **Conceptual Art, Nouveau Realistes, Performance Art, Process Art** and **Sculpto-Pictoramas.**

Hard-Edge Painters (1950s)
These artists, approaching Minimalism, divided the canvas into clearly defined edges and rigid forms, usually without a center of interest. Vivid metallic colors were often used. McLaughlin (1898–1976); Louis (1912–1962); Berman (b. 1912); Kelly (b. 1923); Noland (b. 1924); Youngerman (1926–1962); Indiana (b. 1928); Held (b. 1928); Krushenick (b. 1929); Rockburne (b. 1934); Stella (b. 1936). See **Post-Painterly Abstraction.**

Hard-Edge Painting
Abstract painting based on simple geometric forms painted in two or three cool colors. The surface is treated as a single unit with colors applied in sharp edges. See **Homage to the Square.**

Harlem Renaissance (1920s)
The flowering of black art and literature in the U.S.

Harmony

The blending of tone, color and line to bring about balance; something pleasing to the eye.

Heraldry

Decorative art using armorial insignia or emblems.

Hieroglyphics

1. A form of Egyptian picture writing.
2. Recognizable emblems or symbols used in Renaissance painting.
3. Symbols used by a number of modern artists in their work.

Highlights

1. The brightest lights seen in a picture.
2. That part of an oil painting where the light is most intense, regardless of size.

High Renaissance (1490–1520/1530)

The second phase of the Renaissance when symmetry and the recapture of classical antiquity had reached its fullest expression in the completion of the Sistine Chapel and the Vatican frescoes. The various works of Leonardo da Vinci (1452–1519), Michelangelo (1475–1564) and Raphael (1483–1520) were glorified. Bramante (1444–1514) was the creator of High Renaissance architecture. By this time, the artist was viewed as a supreme genius, which spurred him to inspired goals. Art reached its zenith in Venice, a latecomer to the Renaissance, with the work of Gentile Bellini (1429–1507), Giovanni Bellini (1430–1516) and Carpaccio (1465–1526). The art of Titian (1490–1576) probably represents the high point of 16th century art in Venice. See Mannerism.

Hispanic Art in the U.S.

The term "Hispanic art" is relatively new. The first time it caught the public's attention was in the late 1960s when the Chicano movement in California campaigned for civil rights with their large murals containing political or historical themes. "Los Four"—Lujan (b. 1940), Romero (b. 1941), Almaraz (b. 1941) and Valadez (b. 1951)—thereafter continued the tradition of large paintings of Chicano history and barrio culture in Los Angeles. Other Hispanic artists, who have their roots in the

U.S., Europe or Latin America, have painted and sculpted a great variety of subjects. There is, however, some emphasis on religious themes. Ramirez (1885–1960); Lopez (b. 1942); Sierra (b. 1944); Tapia (b. 1950). As a contrast, several artists have fused Southwestern imagery with Chicanismo. The sculptures of Jimenez (b. 1940) characterize well known types of that region (the cowboy, the pioneer, etc.), while the landscape pictures of Fenandez (b. 1948) reflect on his early life in the Southwest.

Representational art has always dominated Hispanic art, but it has been rendered in diverse ways, as in the satirical, graffiti and cartoon art of Stand (b. 1950), Perez (b. 1951) and Gronk (b. 1954).

As more painters and sculptors migrate to the U.S., they bring with them their traditional themes and styles which meld into their new cultural environment. Buzio (b. 1948); Roche (b. 1955); Gonzalez (b. 1958); among others.

History Painting

Once regarded by academies as the highest and most proper form of art, it has almost disappeared because of photography. The work of the following artists is representative of history painting in the U.S.: Pine (1730–1788); Copley (1738–1815); West (1738–1820) known as the "father" of American painting; J. Peale (1749–1831); Trumbull (1756–1843); H. Sargent (1770–1845); Morse (1791–1872); Weir (1803–1889); Stearns (1810–1885); Leutze (1816–1868); Thompson (1840–1896); MacKenzie (1865–1941); Lovell (b. 1909); among others. See **Revolutionary Art** and **War Paintings.**

Holography

Photographs taken with laser beams which produce three-dimensional images behind or in front of a transparent or reflective surface. It can be viewed from all angles. See **Computer Portrait Sculpture.**

Homage to the Square Series

Albers (1888–1976), a colorist, theorized that every color was affected by the color next to it. His lifelong interest was to make colors do something they don't do by themselves. He proved this theory with a series of paintings wherein he used a simple square-within-a-square format. Albers is known as the "father" of optical art.

Hudson River School (1825–1870s)

A group of New York painters who represented the first American art movement and who specialized in the grandeur of landscape and luminism. The origin of their art lay in romantic literature, and they were proud to be pioneers in showing America's vast, natural and unspoiled beauty. Cole (1801–1848), their spokesman, urged that artists sketch country scenes in open air. Whittredge (1820–1910), Gifford (1823–1880), Church (1826–1900), among others, represented the first generation. The second generation was led by Durand (1796–1886), known as the "father" of American landscape painting, Kensett (1816–1872) and Church. They tended to be more realistic when they copied nature by making careful drawings of details and presenting light in a natural way. The third generation adopted loose brushwork in an attempt to capture the mood of the place. See Landscape, American Impressionism, American Landscape, American Tonalism and Panoramists.

Human Concretions

A term used by Arp (1887–1966) to describe his organic sculptures. He stated that "concretion is something that has grown." See Concrete Art.

Humanism

A popular theory during the Renaissance, which resulted in the gradual introduction of non-religious themes in art. Basically, the theory conceived that man could be his own master through study and research, that "man is the measure of all things." Humanism urged that all philosophical and religious ideas be thought out. It also advanced the growth of personalities as opposed to past anonymity in art.

Hyper-Realism

In Modern Art, the depiction of anything general—a cocktail party, a drugstore window—in photographic reality. The effect is that of lifeless emptiness. See Photo-Realism.

Icon

Usually an object of religious devotion painted on wood panels. It is the best known form of Byzantine art.

Iconography

1. The symbolism or imagery of a body of art to express universal ideas.
2. The imagery used in art.
3. A collection of pictures representing a visual record.

Iconology

The study of icons or artistic symbolism.

Ideal Art

An art based on aesthetic ideals. It grew out of the Greek classical theme with emphasis on a perfectly proportioned human figure. This style remained popular until the 1800s.

Illumination

The art of decorating manuscripts with small designs, scenes, and portraits of the author, including elegant calligraphy whereby the initial letters and opening phrases were enlarged. The illuminations were usually executed in pen and ink or in gouache, frequently highlighted with gold leaf. See **Manuscript Painting** and **Miniature Painting.**

Illusionism

The use of various devices such as shading, perspective, trompe l'oeil, etc. to create the appearance of reality.

Illustration

The artistic representation of an idea, scene or writing.

Illustrator

An artist who is able to capture and interpret the essence of a story and whose work is usually considered unique and original. Illustrators were a great tradition in American art, and many of them were well known and well liked, especially those who illustrated for popular magazines. They continue to flourish. Hughes (1832–1915); Frost (1851–1928); Abbey (1852–1911); Pyle (1853–1911); Sterner (1863–1957); Parrish (1870–1966); Leyendecker (1874–1951); Flagg (1877–1960); Koerner (1878–1938); N. C. Wyeth (1882–1945); Kent (1882-1971); Von Schmidt (1893–

1982); Rockwell (1894–1978); Sundlom (1899–1976); Dohanos (b. 1907); Stahl (1910–1987); Gersten (b. 1927); among others.

Imagery

A collection of forms within a work of art giving expression to the artist's ideas. In Abstract Art, the forms and shapes perceived by the artist.

Impasto

The thick application of paint which often adds character and energy to a painting. Also, the raised decoration on ceramic ware. See **Palette Knife** and **Knife Work.**

Impressionism

A painterly style of painting with its seed first planted by the Barbizon school. It was a unified movement by 1874 and exhibitions were held eight times from that year until 1886. The Impressionists saw the world subjectively and intuitively, according to the sensation of light and movement. They were aware that color changed under light and in interpreting the play of light, the subject became secondary. Essentially, the sensation, not the reality, was the motif. Emphasis was placed on painting everyday scenes directly from nature, alla prima, in contrast to traditional subjects favored by the academicians. These attributes, taken together with the fact that the Impressionists eliminated the most important academic standards of technique, finish and composition, represented a whole re-evaluation of art. Perhaps their greatest achievements were the sensation of liveliness, the liberation of pure, bright colors, freedom of the brushstroke, and the use of a natural optical mixture technique when they introduced the concept of complementary colors (opposite colors on the color wheel), especially in the rendition of shadow which they painted in color. Academic painters of other countries were strongly influenced by the new style. Monet (1840–1926) is known as the "father" of Impressionism; he made hourly studies of the same subject when the quality of shadow and light was analyzed. C. Pissarro (1830–1903); Sisley (1839–1899); Morisot (1841–1895); Renoir (1841–1919); Bazille (1841–1970); Cassatt (1845–1926); Caillebotte (1848–1894); among others. See **Macchiaioli School, Neo-Impressionism, Intimist Painters** and **American Impressionism.**

Imprimitura

In oil painting, a thin transparent glaze applied over a drawing on a white ground as the first coat of color.

Improvisations (1910–1914)

A series of abstract paintings executed by Kandinsky (1866–1944). He attempted to reconcile his nonobjective paintings with supernatural and musical symbols.

Independent Artists, Exhibit of (1910)

The first exhibition in the U.S. without any conditions or prerequisites placed on the artists. It was organized by Henri (1865–1929) and Sloan (1871–1951) to provide opportunities for young artists. Approximately 100 artists, including members of The Eight, exhibited.

Independent Artists, Society of (1917–1941)

This society was formed in New York City for the purpose of creating outlets for modern artists. It was modeled on the French annual Salon des Independants with its mottos of no jury and no prizes. The first exhibition had the work of over 1100 artists represented. Traveling exhibitions and regional shows were encouraged.

Indian Art (500s B.C.–1000 A.D.)

Stonework, metalwork and painting were the major art forms of this culture and were basically related to the themes of sex and religion in harmonious combination. India has produced numerous styles of painting, sculpture and architecture. Sculpture, however, in the form of carvings, reliefs, and free-standing figures played a vital role. The main difference between the temples of various religions was reflected in the sculpture adorning them.

The heart of Hinduism is revelation that is described in poetic metaphors and symbols. The creation of Hindu art was the result of the unison of social and religious groups. It was the belief that every natural being has a spirit which can be invoked by ritual to become visible. Stonework in the form of statues, at first colossal in size, but diminishing in size through the centuries, were essentially iconographic images. The manifestation of multiple arms was symbolic of various powers of that image. The earliest wall painting from 500 A.D. was found in a cave dedicated to the god Vishnu; mural paintings from the 8th and 9th centuries were found in various cave-shrines and temples. Persian techniques in miniature size were introduced by the Muslims, with themes taken from religious stories, myths and epics; woman was commonly the central character.

The Buddhist religion was dominated by architecture, relief sculpture and painting. Ritual cave-shrines from 200–700 A.D. contain non-fresco wall paintings depicting religious rituals, stories of Buddha's previous lives and scenes from everyday life.

The Jaina religion believed in a series of saviors, each of which was reproduced in iconographic statues. A marble ceiling containing hundreds of hand-made sculptured forms representing gods, their attendants, flowers, etc., created in the 11th century in the Vimala Shah temple, is classic of its iconography. Rock-art architecture was modeled on Buddhist work.

From 1000 A.D. to 1500 A.D. various dynasties built magnificent temples in an effort to outdo one another. Regional differences became more defined, but sculpture and architecture remained closely associated. The Muslim invasions caused a decline in the quality and tradition of art. It was not until the Mughal dynasty, under the influence of Europeanism, that art became richer. After the 1700s artists became mere copiers, rather than originators.

Industrial Art a/k/a/ Industrial Design

The design and decoration of useful objects, such as furnishings and appliances.

Infilling

Following the sketch, infilling takes place when the forms and colors are painted onto the outlines.

Infra-Mince

A category invented by Duchamp (1887–1968), meaning "sub-tiny." It referred to wasted energy and was a reaction to the giant, opulent canvases of Modern Art. It was Duchamp's intention that art should be so small as to be almost insignificant.

Ink

India or Chinese ink made from wood or vegetable soot and mixed with animal glue to form a paste. After completion of several other steps, it is then diluted.

In Situ

The creation or repair of a work of art on the site for which it is intended. See Site-Specific Art.

International Gothic a/k/a/ International Style (1375–1425)

During this period the influence of French and Italianate art spread throughout Northern Europe. Ideas were transmitted by artists in their travels: a mutual exchange resulted. Imitating nature became the new style, in contrast to the tradition of relaying the sacred story. After acquiring knowledge of painting the beauty of nature in exquisite, but pseudo-realistic detail, artists became anxious to increase their knowledge of perspective and the form of the human body. The brothers Limbourg (active 1399–1439) are probably the best known artists of this style. See Renaissance.

In The Round

In full sculptured form; three dimensional.

Intimist Painters

Referring to the highly individual Post-Impressionist art of Bonnard (1867–1947) and Vuillard (1868–1940) who adapted some of the methods and colors of Impressionism to interior and close-up scenes of bourgeois life. They were fascinated with subtle variations of light and with radiant, shimmering color. Juxtaposed pattern was their motif: the effect of warmth and intimacy resulted. See Nabis.

Isenheim Altar (1510–1511)

A masterwork executed by Grunewald of the German school. It consists of a polyptych of eleven wings and portrays the most important beliefs of the Christian religion. It is probably one of the greatest works of North European art and is classic of the expressive imagery of Teutonic realism.

Islamic art (600s–1600s)

It was not the art of any particular region or people because the Islamic religion did not identify itself in terms of nationality. Religion, therefore, was the uniting factor. In addition to mosques, monuments and palaces decorated with wall paintings, tile and plasterwork, art was generally represented by the use of rich color, arabesque, intricate pattern, calligraphy, ornamentation—all bound within the spirit of religion. Crafts included lacework, knotted rugs and carpets, metalwork, mosaics, glassware, ivory and wood carvings, and outstanding painted pottery, along with narrative relief and sculpture in the round for wall niches. Manuscript painting was its major pictorial expression: the pictures portrayed a variety of themes, such as hunting scenes, religious rites, romance, legends. Islamic art known as Timurid painting, in particular that of the Herat school, reached its fullest expression in the 1600s. In sum, rather than creating original work, it was the artist's mastery of working within a standard set of conventions that was of prime importance. Muslim craftspersons continue in the crafts of metalwork, carpeting, textiles, etc.

Italianizers or Romanists (1500s–1600s)

Artists from the Low Countries who worked in the Italianate style.

Japanese Art

Its fundamentals:

1. Arts and crafts are related to each other with no real distinction made between them.
2. Presentation and appropriateness.
3. An intense feeling for nature: the recurring theme of the four seasons.
4. A tension between the high art of spirituality and the low art of rich living.

Its major tendencies:

1. Direct imitation of the world (as reflected by the Chinese style of the past 1200 years) and Western influence. Japan has always absorbed foreign influences; its primary models, however, were Chinese calligraphy, ceramics and painting.
2. Poetic imagery whereby Japanese originality and tradition thrive with the expression of beauty, spirituality and harmony.

Japan's contribution to the world of art:

1. The mastery of color prints. Those produced by the Yedo school (1650–1868) through the graphic process of woodcuts were marked by bright colors, bold outlines, simplicity, and blank areas to create the impression of light. When the Japanese resumed trade relations with the West in the 1800s, colorful prints were exported as wrappings, and it was those prints that influenced French artists.
2. The expressionism and reality of sculpture.
3. The craft of pottery continues to produce exciting work, along with lacquer-work, metalwork and textiles. A major breakthrough in Western pottery design occurred when Westerners learned the expressive method of Japanese design.

Beginning in 1868, Japan made westernization and modernization its twin goals. Students began studying in the West and foreigners established colleges and universities in Japan. Art in the present day is a vital force, and while artists are encouraged to learn new styles, their own traditions remain a living power. See Oriental Art.

Japonisme

The influence of Japanese art and design on the Western world.

Junk Art and Sculpture (1950s)

A term first applied to canvases which had attached to them rags, torn reproductions, etc. It was extended to describe assemblages of abstract sculpture from the detritus of machine civilization. Bourgeois (b. 1911); Mallery (b. 1917); Seley (1919–1983); Cesar (b. 1921); Stankiewicz (1922–1983); Chamberlain (b. 1927); Bontecou (b. 1931); DiSuvero (b. 1933); Miki (1937–1977); among others. See Arte Povera and Nouveau Realistes.

Juxtapose, Juxtaposition

1. To place side by side.
2. The combination of colors and shapes.

Kinetic Art and Sculpture

It is basically designed to move or to produce optical illusion. The affirmation of Gabo (1890–1977) that "kinetic rhythm as the basic form of our perception in real time" is reflected in his transparent space sculpture. He renounced color, line, volume and mass as superfluous to reality and espoused a time/space/movement theory. Man Ray (1890–1976); Calder (1898–1976); Rickey (b. 1907); Tomasello (b. 1915); Soto (b. 1923); Takis (b. 1925); Mack (b. 1931); Lijn (b. 1939); among others. See **Constructivism.**

Kineticism

An art form introduced in the 1920s.

1. Optical illusion is exploited through the medium of painting in Op Art.
2. Constructions seem to move along with the spectator.
3. Light strategically placed or directed can create the illusion of movement.
4. Air-powered Mobiles move with the wind.
5. Mechanical parts in Audiokinetic Sculpture cause actual movement.

Kitchen Sink School (1950s)

An English school of Social Realism. Their theme was the drabness and disorder of domesticity. Middleditch (b. 1923); Greaves (b. 1927); J. Smith (b. 1928); Bratby (b. 1928); among others.

Knave of Diamonds (1910–1918)

An important avant-garde and exhibition society in Russia. Besides the work of several Russian painters, they also promoted the work of Cubists, German Expressionists and others. Kandinsky (1866–1944); Malevich (1878–1935); Larionov (1881–1964); Lentulov (1883–1943); Falk (1888–1956); among others.

Knife Work

The use of a palette knife to apply oil paint; the use of a sharp instrument to modify the surface of a watercolor. See **Palette Knife.**

Lacuna

A blank space or a missing part in a painting.

Land Art—See Earth Art.

Landscape

A view of natural inland scenery without a story. For twelve centuries landscape in the Western world was used as a symbolic background. In the Orient, however, landscape was known as a serious form of painting in the 3d century A.D.

The Romans conveyed the sensations of atmosphere, light and space in their representations of background, most notably the illustrations of Homer's "Odyssey" and mural paintings from Casa Livia. Altdorfer (1480–1538) produced one of the first romantic landscapes and is believed to be the predecessor of 17th century landscape artists. Flemish artists in the 1400s/1500s are believed to have brought it to its fullest expression, especially Patinir (1485–1525). Brueghel (1525–1569) is known as one of the great landscape artists of the 16th century. The Carracci family in Italy in the 1600s was a strong influence on the creation of pure landscape. Van Goyen (1596–1656), Cuyp (1620–1691), van Ruisdael (1628–1682) and Hobbema (1638–1709) of the Dutch school are several of the most celebrated landscape artists. In the 1700s/1800s the trend was to represent landscape in a romantic manner. Artists thereafter aimed at the effect of light on nature, which led to Impressionism. During the last decades symbolism in nature seems to be the motif. Several categories of landscape and the artists representative thereof are:

Classical:	Poussin (1594–1665); Claude Lorrain (1600–1682).
Romantic:	Friedrich (1774–1804); Turner (1775–1851); Constable (1776–1837); T. Rousseau (1812–1867); Innes (1825–1894); Bierstadt (1830–1902).
Impressionist:	Sisley (1839–1899); Monet (1840–1926); Sargent (1856–1925); Lawson (1873–1939); Seago (1910–1974).
Surreal:	Miro (1893–1984); Tanguy (1900–1955).
Realistic:	See **American Landscape Art.**
Expressionist:	Whistler (1834–1903); Maurer (1868–1932); Carr (1871–1945); Weber (1881–1961); O'Keefe (1887–1986); Burchfield (1893–1967); Weston (1894–1972); Stamos (b. 1922); Loe (b. 1953).

See Hudson River School, New Romantic Landscape and Mindscape.

Le Blond Ovals

Oval-shaped country scenes using the Baxter Print Process.

Leitmotif

A motif that recurs throughout a design. See Motif.

Life Drawing

The drawing of a live model, usually nude and seated on a raised platform.

Life Mask

A plaster cast molded on the face of the person being portrayed.

Light

The early pioneers of the treatment of light in art were Piero della Francesca (1416–1492) and Masaccio (1401–1428). Another pioneer in the study of light and its values was Claude Lorrain (1600–1682). Delacroix (1798–1863) is credited with associating light and color. Turner (1775–1851) has been considered an influence on generations of artists with his discoveries about the relation of color and light, a major factor of Impressionism whereby the artists used the light of day in shadows and reflections at any given hour to obtain a special atmospheric effect. See Luminism.

Light On

Brightness derived from a specific source, such as natural light falling on objects.

Light Sculpture

The use of fluorescent fixtures to compose reflections and shadows of light in space. Color, light and transparencies became the materials of new sculpture. Flavin (b. 1933); Chryssa (b. 1933); Whitman (b. 1935); Bell (b. 1939); among others. See Zero Group.

Light Through

This is illustrated by a stained glass window through which light flows and by paintings whose light seems to come toward us through the object portrayed.

Limited Edition

A term used in printmaking to restrict the number of reproductions to be made. It usually indicates a fine quality reproduction of an original painting. See **Multiples** and **Printmaking.**

Limners (also called "face painters")

Those untrained Early American portraitists who lacked technical competence possessed a strong sense of observation and imagination. Their folk-like style had the effect of naivety and charm. A great number of them earned their living travelling from town to town recording portraits of those who could pay for their services. Phillips (1788–1865); Johnston (active 1796–1824); S. Shute (1803–1836); R. Shute (1803–1882); Field (1805–1900); Prior (1806–1873); Stock (1815–1855); Hamblin (active 1823–1856); Bradley (active 1837–1845); among others. See **Portraiture.**

Limning—See Miniature Painting.

Line (A mark one inch or longer)

The real or imaginary outline of any representation made by an artist according to his perception; an outline or a contour. The action or quality of the line can carry the artist's meaning. A few examples are:

-Angular	Stiffness in character and manner; somber
-Bold	Strength; drama
-Curvilinear	Decorative
-Delicate	Soft, tender
-Diagonal	Movement; dynamism
-Horizontal	Calmness
-Overlapping	Illusion of forms
-Serried	Crowded; pressed together
-Vertical	Tension; sadness

Line and Wash Drawings

An outline usually in ink that is shaded by watercolor or diluted ink. This technique was known of in antiquity and was popular during the Baroque period.

Linear

An emphasis on contour and outline.

Line Drawing

The depiction of a subject according to the seemingly calligraphic quality or property of the line. Etching is considered a good process for the production of line drawings.

Literary Art

1. The subject is taken from a story.
2. A form of illustrative or narrative art.

Little Masters

1. A title given to genre painters of the Dutch school. Each of those artists seemed to have a specialty.
2. A title given to Greek vase painters.

Loaded

A picture full of color executed with a loaded brush.

Luminism

An effect obtained when light is visible through an outer layer of paint. Bingham (1811–1879) in particular was a leading exponent of luminism when this technique was developed in the 1800s in the U.S. Artists portrayed landscape realistically, but with a heavenly glowing effect. See **American Landscape** and **Hudson River School.**

Luna Luna (1987–1989)

An international art amusement park conceived by the Viennese artist-inventor Heller (b. 1947) who wants to bring a museum of art to the people. Many well known artists, such as Appel, Baselitz, Basquiat, Beuys, Delaunay, Dali, Haring, Kiefer, Lichtenstein and Scharf, have contributed to the wondrous presentation of sights and sounds.

Lyrical Abstraction (Abstract Lyrique)

A style that is characterized with a casual, informal and psychic approach. It is expressive of a floating sensation. Richards (1903–1971); Ferren (1905–1970); Frankenthaler (b. 1928); Natkin (b. 1930); Williams (1934–1988); among others. See **Art Informel.**

Macchiaioli School (1850–1900)

A pre-Impressionist movement formed in Florence. The artists painted in the open air to record their impressions of informal subjects. They applied paint to the canvas in patches and dabs. Fattori (1825–1908); Signorini (1835–1901); Cecioni (1838–1886); Bianchi (1840–1904); among others.

Machines

A term used to describe large size or monumental paintings.

Macrame

The art of creative knotwork was popular as a nautical pastime in the 1800s. In recent decades, however, it has enjoyed a comeback as a craft in the U.S.

Magic Realism

1. The Cave Art of imaginary scenes with the hope that a psychic union would be made between the painting and the real object.
2. Paintings characterized by a naturalistic style with objects produced in almost clinical detail. Spilimbergo (1896–1964); Shahn (1898–1969); Kovner (b. 1915); A. Wyeth (b. 1917); among others.
3. The creation of mystery through strange, disturbing juxtapositions. Roy (1880–1950), its "father"; Delvaux (1897–1944); Balthus (b. 1904); among others.

Maniera Greca (in the Greek manner)

The style used in Italianate painting in the 1200s, which was influenced by Byzantine painting.

Manner

The "handwriting" or style of an artist. The modern use of "in a mannered style" is considered disparaging.

Mannerism (1530–1590)

The reactionary style of European artists (sometimes called "anti-classicists") who may perhaps be called the first of the modern artists because they broke away from the traditional harmony and balance of Renaissance painting when they distorted the human figure and used harsh coloring and lighting. Social and political conditions were influential on the development of

Mannerism but, in the main, it was the result of artists working out new ideas. Romano (1499–1546); Parmigianino (1503–1540); Dell'Abbate (1512–1571); Tintoretto (1518–1594); El Greco (1541–1614); among others. See **Baroque.**

Manuscript Painting

The unique art of painting handwritten books. This art form was known of in Egypt and other cultures; it reached its fullest expression in the Western world during the Romanesque and Gothic periods. The introduction of printing saw its rapid decline. See **Illumination and Miniature Painting.**

Maquette

A small sculpture in wax or clay made as a preliminary model for the client's approval.

Marbling

The art of imitating marble patterns on solid surfaces. It was popular from the 17th through the 19th centuries. In current use, it is considered a craft.

Marine Painting

The depiction of ship portraits, shore scenes, genre scenes of commerce or harbor activity, yacht races, etc. In rendering ship portraits the artist painted every detail accurately because the client would not tolerate anything but exact representation. In so doing, ship portraits have become important to historians, especially those representations of steamboats and sailboats by John Bard (1815–1856) and James Bard (1815–1897). Salmon (1775–1844); Birch (1779–1851); Lane (1804–1865); Bonfield (1805–1898); Richards (1833–1905); Silva (1835–1886); Jacobsen (1850–1921); Symons (1861–1930); F. J. Waugh (1861–1940); Jack W. Smith (1873–1949); Grant (1875–1962); Fischer (1882–1962); among others. See **Seascape Painting.**

Mark-Making

Referring to the making of marks one inch or shorter.

Masses

The representation of the basic shapes of groups.

Master Painter

Under the guild system, one who was entitled to practice art on his own. Also, one so highly skilled that he employs assistants or has students.

Masterpiece/Masterwork

1. A work of art done with extraordinary skill.
2. A work of art presented to a medieval guild to qualify for the rank of master.

Material Pictures

A technique peculiar to Nesch (1893–1975) who was influenced by German Expressionism. He created mosaic-like constructions with wire, mesh, colored glass, nails, etc. that were affixed to printing plates.

Matte

A dull surface produced by lean colors; without gloss or shine.

Matterism

A style of painting in Belgium and in the Netherlands wherein the artist used heavy impasto embodied with found objects. Wagemaker (1906–1972); Mendelson (b. 1915); Bogart (b. 1921); among others.

Medieval Art

Its major theme was the relationship between time and the eternal. See **Middle Ages.**

Mediterranean Art

—The non-Greek Minoan Culture (3400–1100 B.C.) sited on Crete, the first civilization in Europe, was highly developed. Metalwork, including fine jewelry, fresco painting, miniature sculpture and the decorative arts, all characterized by a freedom of style, were the key arts and crafts.

—The Mycenaean Culture (1600–1100 B.C.) was a warrior-structured society located in the Aegean area. Based on an unsophisticated version of the Minoan world, their art consisted of metalwork, pottery, gold death masks and fresco painting. The Dark Ages followed. See **Greek Art.**

Medium
1. The type of paint an artist uses. In a more specific sense, it refers to the vehicle or the binder for the paint being used.
2. A tool or material used by an artist.
3. The method of expression used: the Graphic Arts, painting, etc.

Memento Mori (Remember, you must die)
An object used in art as a reminder of death. See Vanitas.

Mesopotamian Art (3500–1000 B.C.)
With the exception of royal graves, highly decorative architecture and statuary in the service of the gods, little is known of this area corresponding to modern Iraq. It was inhabited by many cultures through the centuries and has been called "the Cradle of Man." Art was realistically or symbolically expressive. They excelled in narrative relief, metalwork and the carving of gemstones and bronzes. Kings often commissioned monuments to commemorate victories in war or royal hunts.

Metaphysical School (1915–1920)
A school founded by Carra (1881–1966), deChirico (1888–1978), Morandi (1890–1964), and DePisis (1896–1956) in Italy. They painted surrealistic pictures expressive of those things that exist beyond the known and real world. See Surrealism.

Metier
An artist's forte or special interest.

Mezzotint Prototypes (an English tone process of engraving)
These prototypes were popularly used as models by Early American artists. Patroon painters had collections of them so that their patrons could choose the desired pose and costume.

Middle Ages (500–1500)
A term first used to describe the medieval period. Religion was the dominating force in life and art. The early Middle Ages represented the first age of Europe when the culture of the modern world was formulated with the establishment of universities, political institutions, national identity, growth of Catholic Christendom, etc. Arts and crafts endemic to those centuries consisted primarily of fresco painting, illuminated manuscripts,

relief sculpture, tapestries and stained glass, all representative of aesthetic and religious values.

Middle Distance

A term used in landscape painting to define a level surface behind the foreground.

Mindscape

A term coined by Wright (b. 1948) for his painted landscapes. His premise is that when one reads poetry repeatedly, it becomes a part of one's inner self. This theory is applied to his paintings when he translates his own conception of the spiritual or psychological essence of nature, as well as its beauty, onto a surface without actually copying from nature. He uses a mixed media.

Miniature Painting

A term used to describe several styles of painting, usually portraiture.

1. Illuminated manuscripts.
2. Small size portraits and medallions by specialists in Europe from the 1600s to the 1800s. They were known as "paintings in little." Hilliard (1547–1619); Cooper (1609–1672); Cosway (1742–1821); among others.
3. Small size portraits in the U.S. called "limnings."

Miniature painting is a direct descendant of manuscript illumination. Although its popularity waned with the invention of photography, several American artists excelled. C. W. Peale (1741–1827); J. Peale (1749–1831); Malbone (1777–1807); A. C. Peale (1791–1878).

Minimalism (1960s–1970s)

Basically, the reduction of art to its barest essentials; a purified, simple, geometric and sculptural art. Its emphasis is on the inner nature of objects. Goeritz(b. 1915); Caro (b. 1924); Judd (b. 1928); LeWitt (b. 1928); Morris (b. 1931); Andre (b. 1935); Tucker (b. 1935); Serra (b. 1939); Johanson (b. 1940); among others. Minimalist painters who rendered large fields of monochromes include A. Martin (b. 1912); Ryman (b. 1930); Rockburne (b. 1934); Barden (b. 1938); among others. See Hard-Edge Painters and Primary Structures.

Minor Arts

A special group that involves the use of solid materials, such as textiles, glass, wood and gems, to produce useful items.

Mirror Painting

A technique peculiar to Pistoletto (b. 1933) whereby he traced a series of life size photographs in arrested movement onto transparent paper and then cut out and pasted them onto sheets of polished steel. They were painted in sombre colors. The steel sheets were arranged to reflect the image of the viewer.

Mixed Media

The use of different materials in the same work of art. See **Multi-Media.**

Mixed Method

Oil over tempera underpainting.

Mobile

A term specifically ascribed to the hanging sculptures of Calder (1898–1976) which he began to create in the 1930s. They were made of metal rods, wire, glass, plastic, etc. and arranged in inventive forms. Calder wanted to balance the movement of colored forms with air current, giving the effect of airborne sculptures. He said, "When everything goes right, a mobile is a piece of poetry that dances with the joy of life and surprises." Calder developed a new form of expression in Modern Art. See **Stabile, Kineticism and Kinetic Art and Sculpture.**

Model

1. A person who poses for an artist.
2. An object that is studied by an artist.
3. A representation of something.
4. To shape or build up with plastic material.

Modello or Modelletto

When a painting was commissioned in centuries past, the artist would often make a small version of it for the patron's approval.

Modern Art

Throughout its history, Modern Art has initiated dozens of styles. A common theme is the artist's desire to simplify and to get down to basics. In each of its movements, the style most often reflects a reaction to an earlier style. Essentially, Modern Art's major approaches are (1) self-expression and experimentation and (2) the desire for harmony through a systematic but intuitive arrangement. Matisse's (1869–1954) statement that "Exactitude is not truth" seems to embody the thesis of Modern Art.

Several pioneers of Modern Art were:

—Manet (1832–1883) He was considered a revolutionary because he painted life as it appeared to his senses, without disguise, and without using conventional methods. Manet used bold, contrasting colors side by side. It is believed that the contemporary age of painting is reflected through Manet's technique and use of colors. He was closely allied with the Impressionists and has been called "a painter's painter."

—Cezanne (1839–1906) He is known as the "father" of Modern Art because it was his intention to see the world objectively. He wanted to maintain the vitality and character of the subject—without using perspective. He did so by painting in daubs of colors to create mass, rather than using the traditional technique of modelling from dark and light. In so doing, he was able to reduce structures. He then proceeded to build his pictures with these simplified elements to re-create form and space, enabling viewers to see depth and volume. Cezanne referred to his work as "constructions after nature."

-Gauguin (1848–1903) He used large areas of flat color. His figures and landscapes transcend reality and symbolize spiritual and universal themes.

—van Gogh (1853–1890) He made known his inner feelings with expressive, pulsating brushwork and brilliant, radiant and decorative colors. Color was his language. His work was influential in the formation of Fauvism and Expressionism.

—Munch (1863–1944) The first modern painter to study the personality. He was concerned with humanity, inner visions and dreams. His work served as a catalyst between Neo-Impressionism and Expressionism.

—Kandinsky (1866–1944) and Klee (1879–1940) Their discoveries, innovations and writings were influential on the development of Modern Art. Klee's summation of its purpose was "not to reflect the visible, but to make visible."

—Leger (1881–1955) The machine was a great influence on his work. He was one of the first artists whose paintings focused on modern urban life with the portrayal of solid machine-like structures in flat colors with dark outlines. He thought that "beauty is everywhere."

—Picasso (1881–1973) The master of the modern school of Paris, whose range of skills from painting to theatre design gives his genius the same place in the 20th century as Giotto in the Middle Ages and Michelangelo during the Renaissance. Picasso's "Demoiselles d'Avignon" (1907) can be considered the first 20th century painting. See **Twentieth Century Art.**

Modernism

The theory of Modern Art rejecting past styles.

Moire

The optical illusion obtained when two geometric designs are superimposed.

Monochrome Picture

A picture executed in various tones of one color.

Monolith

A single but huge stonepiece shaped into a sculptural form, such as an obelisk or a column.

Montage

A composite picture resulting from the placing of objects, materials, prints or photographs in a preconceived design to produce comical, convulsive or lyrical fantasies. See **Photomontage.**

Monumental

A grand size; bigger than life.

Morellian Principles

These were formulated to study the minute details of a painting to reveal the "handwriting" of the artist, a method used to detect counterfeit work.

Mosaic

A method of decoration using small pieces of colored glass, stone or ceramics which are inlaid on a background to form a design or a picture. This craft was known in ancient Egypt, Greece, Islam and in Eastern Christendom. The mosaic work found in the churches located in Ravenna and Venice is classic.

Motif

1. A dominant feature or recurring theme.
2. A single or recurring design or color.
3. An influence.
4. The subject or theme of a work of art.

Motion

The creation of movement in paintings includes the following dynamics:

1. Arrested or inactive, usually seen in two-dimensional paintings.
2. Free, whereby movement is liberated by the deep space of perspective.
3. The stroboscopic effect of successive stages in a single image or the after-image of a moving object produced by blurring, streaking, etc.
4. A change in measurable quality, such as size, hue, brightness, etc.
5. Eye-movement.

Motion or Mood Studies

A term used by Tack (1870–1949) to describe his process. He enlarged photos of the desert so that realistic images would disappear. He then traced the outlines onto canvas and painted with rich colors. According to his understanding, the language of color symbolized the mysteries of nature, the emotions, and God.

Mount

1. To arrange or assemble for display.
2. The material on which a picture is placed.

Mourning Pictures

An American Folk Art going back to the death of George Washington and continuing into the 1800s. The symbols of death are included: tomb, graveyard, mourners, etc.

Movement

Rhythmic action or flow running through a picture. See **Motion.**

Muddiness

The overuse of pigment, giving a muddy appearance.

Multi-Media

The combination of various art forms in the creation of a painting or other artistic endeavor.

Multiples

A term used to describe Graphic Arts and cast sculptures that are produced in unlimited numbers—the opposite of Limited Edition.

Mural

A large work of art painted on a wall or on a canvas or panel for mounting on a wall. The work of Mexican artists Orozco (1883–1949), Rivera (1886–1957), Siqueiros (1896–1974) and Tamayo (b. 1899) is classic of mural work in the modern age. More recently, however, this style has become a popular form of expression in inner-city neighborhoods. These murals focus on the lives, problems and culture of the people. Frequently the artists are urged to create murals only after they have determined the subject, design and production in collaboration with residents. In essence, these murals are billboards that tell a community's story. See **Hispanic Art in the U.S.**

Museum

An institution dedicated to the collection, care, study and display of works of art, history and natural science as objects of lasting value or interest.

Mythological Painting (1400s–1800s)

The painting of stories or allegorical narrative involving supernatural elements. The seven paintings of Titian (1490–1576) called "poesie" (poetries), including the "The Rape of Europe," are classic of the mythological theme.

Nabis, Les (Prophets in Hebrew)(1889–1899)

A group of friends who possessed diverse talents in the arts. Their main links were their educational and family backgrounds. The painters among them were influenced by Gauguin's flat colors and Denis's arrangement of colors and harmony of forms. Several of them produced compositions which indicated their interest in occultism, using sacred or occult symbols as their iconographic language. Serusier (1863–1927); Ranson (1864–1909); Vallatton (1865–1925); Ibels (1867–1936); Roussel (1867–1944); Bonnard (1867–1947); Vuillard (1868–1940). See **Intimist Painters** and **Symbolism**.

Naive Art (Naif)

An art that is marked by simplicity and naturalism untouched by popular style. The portrayal of subjects is not representational or realistic. The artist is usually self-taught. Humor, reality, sophistication and innocence are four of its common themes. H. Rousseau (1844–1910); Kane (1860–1934); "Granma" Moses (1860–1961); Metelli (1872–1938); Hirshfield (1872–1946); Lagru (1873–1960); Bombois (1883–1970); Pippin (1888–1946); Ottone (1895–1957); Ferrara (b. 1906); Muth (b. 1919); M. Delacroix (b. 1933); among others.

Narrative Art

The relating of a story in a series of events or in a decisive moment. From Early Christian years through the Renaissance, relaying the sacred story was the major narrative theme. One of the most remarkable narrative renditions is that of "The Battle of Alexander and Darius" by Altdorfer (1480–1538). Hogarth (1697–1764) and Greuze (1725–1805) are known for their morality themes. Krimmel (1787–1821) painted hundreds of humorous or eventful scenes of American life. In Modern Art, narrative uses simple imagery to act out a story.

National Academy of Design

The most important American art institution in the 1800s. It was founded in 1826 in reaction to the conservative policies of the American Academy of Fine Art. Its formation was influential in creating New York City as the center for American art. In time, however, many members became dissatisfied with its policies and formed the Society of American Artists in 1877. Thereafter, in the 20th century, the development of American contemporary art and Modern Art took place outside of academy walls. See The Eight and 291 Group.

Natural History Art—See Wildlife and Natural History.

Naturalism

A representation giving the effect of accuracy without creating the illusion of reality, as rendered in Naive or Primitive Art.

Nazarenes (early 1800s)

A group of German painters who were inspired by the work of Italian fresco painters of the Early Renaissance. Art, in their opinion, was a religious mission. They sought a romantic purity to revitalize the "soul" of the German state. Their work was produced in a flat, archaic style, using light tones. van Cornelius (1783–1865); Pforr (1788–1812); Overbeck (1789–1869); Begas (1794–1854); Schnorr (1795–1872).

Neo-Abstraction (1980s)

The nonrepresentational, independent work of artists who have a wide range of attitudes toward art and who seem to have re-invented the language of abstraction. The artists use any style they like for this new "vocabulary." Reed (b. 1946), an exponent of this group, stated: "People do not know what abstraction should be, and so it can be any number of things." Hodgkin (b. 1932), another exponent, stated: "To be an artist now, you have to make your own language. . . ." Richter (b.1932); Murray (b. 1940); Scully (b.1945); Jensen (b. 1945); Janovich (b. 1948); Laufer (b. 1950); Schuyff (b. 1958); among others. Its sculptors include Burton (b. 1939); Graves (b. 1940); Winsor (b. 1941); Puryear (b. 1941); Lipski (b. 1947); Deacon (b. 1949); among others.

Neoclassicism

A style of painting, sculpture and architecture emerging in France during the period of the Enlightenment. Artists reacted against the frivolity of ornate Baroque-Rococo by calling for a return to order, reason and discipline. They modeled their work on classical form, but used contemporary events as their subjects. David (1748–1825); Gerard (1770–1837); Gros (1771–1835); Guerin (1774–1833); Ingres (1780–1867); among others. See Romanticism.

Neo-Dada

A term embracing non-traditional art forms, such as Pop Art, Nouveau Realisme, Assemblage, etc.

Neo-Expressionism (sometimes referred to as Neo-Figuration) (late 1970s–1980s)

A generic term for postmodern art in which angst-ridden emotionalism and freely-expressive brushwork are emphasized. Stimulating imagery and figural representations are appropriated from older, non-traditional art and the media. Typical are Bosman (b. 1944) who paints catastrophic themes; Chia (b. 1946) who paints scenes depicting the details of everyday life, daydreams and violent themes; Salle (b. 1952) who exploits nude figuration; Cabo (b. 1952) who paints allegories of creation. Other Neo-Expressionists include Gordillo (b. 1934); Baselitz (b. 1938); Lupertz (b. 1941), Polke (b. 1941); Immendorf (b. 1945); Kiefer (b. 1945); Fischl (b. 1948); Schnabel (b. 1951); among others. Perhaps the many German representatives indicates a connection with that country's troubled history.

Neo-Geo (1980s)

Two of its approaches are Geometric Abstraction and a mixed media. It has been referred to by several names, but Halley (b. 1953), one of its exponents, prefers "Simulationism" because natural things have been replaced by technical mediums: movies in place of life; bio-mechanical control of life, etc. The only source of commonality among the artists is the depiction of images rather than original sources; they feel that the world totally consists of images. It seems to indicate a deadness of culture. Levine (b. 1947); Bleckner (b. 1949); Beckerton (b. 1950); Young (b. 1952); Taaffe (b. 1955); among others.

Neo-Impressionism a/k/a Pointillism or Divisionism

A short-lived movement of the late 1800s initiated by Seurat (1859–1891) who wanted to transform Impressionism with the scientific breakdown or division of primary colors in nature to paint them methodically onto canvas as tiny strokes or dots, resulting in a flat, geometric appearance. In order to reconstitute the image into a field of action, the viewer would have to step back. See Optical Mixture. Seurat cared mostly about color and pattern and his purpose in painting was to bring about "an act of harmony." Cross (1856–1910); Luce (1858–1941); Signac

(1863–1935); van de Velde (1863–1957); Hayet (1864–1940). See Post-Impressionists.

Neolithic
1. Belonging to an earlier age and now obsolete.
2. Referring to the last stage of the Stone Age.

Neo-Plasticism
The style of the DeStijl movement which expressed a desire for complete objectivity. Mondrian (1872–1944) created its theme: simplicity and no illusion. He wanted to portray the harmony of the universe by using vertical and horizontal lines; he used only primary colors and black and white.

Neo-Realism (1913–1914)
A philosophy developed by English artists Gilman (1876–1919), Gore (1878–1914) and Ginner (1878–1952) whereby they thought that Realism should be created on canvas in accordance with the artist's interpretation of nature, a belief similar to that of the Impressionists.

Neo-Romanticism (late 1920s–1930s)
A movement whose themes of sadness, mystery and fantasy seemed to represent a sort of psychological escapism. The artists sought lyrical qualities and a return to man and his environment without distortion. L. Berman (1896–1976); Tchelitchew (1898–1957); E. Berman (1899–1972); Berard (1902–1949); among others.

Netherlandisch School—See Flemish School.

New Artists Alliance (Neu Kunstlervereiningung a/k/a/ NKV)
A reaction to Realism by a group of Expressionists formed in Munich in 1909. They wanted to experiment without restriction with the inner world and with impressions received from nature. A search was made for nothing but the essentials. It gradually became a force for all modern European artists. (Several members resigned in 1911 to form The Blue Rider.) Jawlensky (1864–1941); Kandinsky (1866–1944); Munter (1877–1962); Marc (1880–1916); among others.

New English Art Club (1886–1916)
This association was founded by Sargent (1856–1925) and

others whose paintings were representative of contemporary, progressive art. Naturalistic painting was their motif. They wanted to follow "the methods long practiced in France—vivid and simple study of nature." F. Brown (1851–1941); Lavery (1856–1941); Guthrie (1859–1930); Gore (1878–1914); John (1878–1961); P. Nash (1889–1946); Steer (1890–1943); among others.

New Hope School (1898–1930s)

These countryside landscape painters were inclined toward Impressionism. They were considered the rural counterpart of the Ashcan School who were their contemporaries. Lathrop (1859–1938) was the founder of this Bucks County group near the Delaware River, and Redfield (1869–1965) was its acknowledged leader. Spencer (1879–1931); Sotter (1879–1953); Garber (1880–1958); Bredin (1881–1933); Baum (1884–1956); Leith-Ross (1886–1973); Coppedge (1888–1951); among others.

New Image Painting and Sculpture (1970s)

A new label for a number of artists who had little in common and who denied the existence of any movement other than their interest in renewing the art of painting, with imagery as their motif. The new images created were often flat figural outlines set against deep or monochromatic colors that were painted or constructed with eccentric or whimsical touches. Moskowitz (b. 1935); Bartlett (b. 1941); Zucker (b. 1941); Borofsky (b. 1942); Jenney (b. 1945); Rothenberg (b. 1945); Africano (b. 1948); Sultan (b. 1951); among others. Its sculptors: Burton (b. 1939); Shapiro (b. 1941); Flanagan (b. 1941); among others. See Neo-Geo.

New Objectivity, The (die Neue Sachlichkeit) (1920s–1930s)

A German reactionary outgrowth. The artists used harsh verism to portray current social evils; their work was satirical, cynical and emotional in theme. Beckmann (1884–1950); Kokoschka (1886–1980); Dix (1891–1969); Grosz (1893–1959).

New Realism (1950s–1970s)

A super realistic, figural but impersonal and objective style, as seen in the work of Pearlstein (b. 1924) and Arikha (b. 1929) or as seen in Photo-Realism or Super Realism. Its dominant feature is to create the illusion of a photograph.

New Romantic Landscape (1980s)

The return to landscape painting may be an indication of artistic reaction to the recent focus on man-made objects and imagery. In its new format, however, the conventions of representation are no longer used to depict the environment but, instead, fragmented landscapes are expressed in inventive abstractions. No sense of the rational seems to exist because of the highly unique concepts of landscape and the materials used. Deutch (b. 1943); Goldstein (b. 1945); Jenney (b. 1945); Ess (b. 1946); Hansell (b. 1947); Blair (b. 1952); Gornick (b. 1953); Joyce (b. 1956); Innerst (b. 1957); Beerman (b. 1958); Trayson (b. 1960); among others.

New York School—See Abstract Expressionism.

Nonfigurative Art
Nonobjective Art
Nonrepresentational Art

Generally, the arrangement of forms and colors not intended to represent an actual object or any element in nature. Specifically, in nonobjective art, forms, lines, colors and textures are manipulated for their own sake.

North American Indian and Eskimo Art

The making of crafts was an integral part of Indian life. Technical proficiency and productivity were the criteria for prestige rather than originality in color and design. Form usually followed function. Gradually, however, decorative elements developed in the production of such articles as mocassins, blankets, clothing, with symbols of prestige, religion or mythology. Painting was important in the decoration of pottery and clothing. Sand painting connected to healing was practiced by the Navajo tribe. Some of the well known Indian crafts are basket-weaving, embroidery, the making of silver and turquoise jewelry, woven articles, ceremonial artifacts, textiles, pottery, carving, and the use of beads as decorative items.

Eskimo arts and crafts were closely related to the struggle for survival. They are represented by small ivory sculptures, harpoonweights, masks and utilitarian objects made from driftwood. The craft of sculptured artifacts increased in popularity so that in recent centuries they became objects sold as souvenirs.

As in Indian culture, Eskimo art depended on the materials

available, and in those areas where wood was available, wood-carving became a major craft.

In the modern world, Indians have adopted the art forms of painting, drawing and printmaking and have renewed the crafts of carving and costume-making for traditional reasons and for commercial purposes. See Primitive Art.

North European Art (sometimes referred to as the Northern Renaissance)

Flemish painting (Belgium and the Netherlands)

—1300s Artists were generally informed about advances made by Italian artists. During this century, most of the art consisted of manuscript illumination.

—1400s The Master of Flemalle (a/k/a Robert Campin) is considered one of the great artists of this period. The painting of the "Ghent Altarpiece" by the brothers van Eyck illustrates a great change. The representation of detail is extraordinary. With the exceptional representation of reality, these artists became perfect eyewitnesses to history. "The Betrothal of Arnolofini" (1434) by Jan van Eyck is classic of this manifestation. The technical contributions of the van Eycks, including the perfection of oil painting, were a direct cause of the revolution of art.

—1500s With his depiction of man's activities, Brueghel demonstrated a strong trend to secular art. The work of Massys is considered a bridge between the work of the van Eycks and Rubens, the last of the great Flemish artists.

—1600s The Netherlands produced the major painters of Northern Europe.

German painting (Austria, Switzerland, etc.)

—1300s The influence of foreign and medieval art was strong. Teutonic realism, however, remained the motif for centuries.

—1400s The invention of the Graphic Arts launched an economical method to supply the populace with woodcuts, playing cards and book-blocks. The mastery of technical problems was seen in the work of several artists of the German school.

—1500s Despite knowledge of Renaissance painting, it was not generally assimilated. Peasant genre with disquieting expression was preferred. Painting was perfected to a high degree in the work of Altdorfer, Baldung-Grien, Durer and Grunewald.

French painting

—1400s The development of a distinctly French style was

reflected in the painting of portraits and in manuscript illumination.

—1500s By mid-century the beginnings of the Renaissance could be seen in a courtly style after Francis I had commissioned Italian artists. A Franco/Italianate style developed in architecture. An important contribution to French Renaissance painting was the portrait.

North Light

The exposure most favored by artists because of its stability.

Nouveau Realistes (1960s)

A group of artists led by the French critic Pierre Restany who promoted a philosophy of "sociological reality" that resulted in the random collection of artifacts and junk which were converted into nonrational assemblages. The theme seemed to be the reduction of an argument to an absurdity. Rotella (b. 1918); Cesar (b. 1921); Tinguely (b. 1925); Klein (1928–1962); Arman (b. 1928); Christo (b. 1935); Raysse (b. 1936); among others.

Novecento Italiano (1920s)

A movement that rejected avant-garde art. It was Italy's version of a return to order. The artists wanted to paint in a naturalistic style based on Renaissance tradition. They were determined to cast off all imported influences. Marussig (1879–1937); Sironi (1885–1961); Bucci (1887–1955); Oppi (1889–1947); among others.

November Group, The (die Novembergruppe)

A movement formed in Berlin in 1918 by C. Klein (1876–1954) and Peckstein (1881–1955). They were concerned with reconstruction and the fine arts, and it was their hope to bring about a close relation between artists and the public. The movement became too large and split into two segments: one that wanted to participate in the social struggle through Realism which led to the formation of the New Objectivity; the second group wanted to participate in the exploration of their own souls which eventually led to Surrealism. Mueller (1874–1930); Purrman (1880–1966); Campendock (1889–1957); among others.

Nude Art

In the Greek classical era, sculptors idealized the human form so much that their creations in perfect proportions seemed almost divine. Under the humanist phase of the Renaissance, a resurgence of the nude form was seen in the paintings of several master artists. Since that rediscovery, Western artists have continued to use the nude in various ways. In Modern Art, however, the nude is portrayed according to the non-classical tradition of expression peculiar to the 20th century artist. Degas (1834–1917); Renoir (1841–1919); Bonnard (1867–1947); Matisse (1869–1954); Genth (1876–1953); Modigliani (1884–1920); Freud (b. 1922); Pearlstein (b. 1924); Wesselmann (b. 1931); Ramos (b. 1935); among others.

Nude Descending a Staircase (2nd version, 1912) by Duchamp (1887–1967)

This painting, as one of the first examples of Modern Art seen in the U.S., created a furor at the Armory Show in 1913. It was executed in multiple images with the intention of portraying movement. It was Duchamp's personal version of Cubism.

Objective Painting

An attempt to reconstruct the world as seen in its reality, in contrast to abstract or nonobjective painting.

Objet d'Art

A curio; any object having artistic value.

Oceanic Art

Art of the South Pacific.

Oeuvre

A French term referring to the lifework of an artist.

Oil Paint

A pigment is mixed with a drying agent and an oil.

Oleograph

A print resembling an oil painting.

Op Art (1960s–1970s)

Its basic premise is that the eye can be tricked because of optical illusion where color contrasts are juxtaposed. Essentially, Op Art is based on pattern perception and the sense of it can only be completed by the viewer. One technique creates after-images or an illusion through intense color and geometric patterns; another technique uses the effects of light and shade. Whatever technique, an effect on the retina results, sometimes to the detriment of the spectator. Vasarely (b. 1908), the "father of Op"; Soto (b. 1923); Agam (b. 1928); Anuszkiewicz (b. 1930); Riley (b. 1931); Poons (b. 1937); Bell (b. 1939); among others.

Open Edition—See Multiples.

Opening

A private showing of an exhibition, usually a day or two prior to opening for the public.

Optical Mixture

A color theory involving the analysis of light and color and their interaction, a laborious and time-consuming process. Colors in tiny specks and dots (the "splitting of color") are applied to the canvas which fuse in the viewer's eye from a distance. See Neo-Impressionism.

Order

An arrangement or sequence.

Organic

A living force; movement; a natural and free flow.

Oriental Art

Its common art objects are handscrolls, hanging scrolls, silk fans, folding fans, album painting, screens. See **Chinese Art** and **Japanese Art**.

Original Art

1. An artist's creation.
2. A prototype from which copies or reproductions are made.

Ornament

A decoration or decorative object: something that gives beauty.

Orphism a/k/a Orphic Cubism (1911–1913)

The art of painting new abstract geometric forms, essentially non-existent structures, in vivid colors. The artists sought to express a state of consciousness through painting to induce the viewer to contemplate oneness with the universe. They saw the world as a composition of dynamic forces which led them to paint abstractions of line and color. Kupka (1871–1957); Bruce (1880–1937); Leger (1881–1955); Weber (1881–1961); Delaunay (1885–1941) among others. See **Synchromism**.

Ottonian Renaissance (919–1060)

This revival took place in Germany under the Ottos and the Henrys. It was marked by exceptional manuscript illumination executed in a lively and expressive manner. Work in wood, ivory, gold and silver was outstanding.

Outline

A line defining the shape of an object.

Overpainting

The top layer of pigment applied to an underpainting.

Paint

A pigment dispersed in a medium.

Painterly

1. The definition or expression of form by the merging of color and tone.
2. The blurred or soft-edge definition of color and contour, in contrast to hard-edge painting.
3. Referring to painting in which all elements are in accordance with technical and aesthetic standards.

Painting

The use by artists of different mediums, usually on a flat surface, to create an image according to the artist's conception or perception.

Palette

1. The complete set of colors for use in the technique, method or medium of painting.
2. A wooden tray-like structure designed to hold paints and brushes.
3. Refer to Color Vocabulary.

Palette Knife

A tool, the working end of which is flat and pointed, used especially for applying thick layers of paint. See **Impasto**.

Panel Painting

Painting on a wood or metal panel.

Panorama

An all-inclusive view of a wide landscape or a continuous landscape arranged around a room or other space. It was a popular style for the depiction of battle scenes of the Civil War and of American views, such as Niagara Falls.

Panoramists

American painters who wanted to create majestic renditions of landscape. See **Hudson River School**.

Papier Collé (Pasted Paper)

A variety of collage invented by Braque and Picasso in 1913 wherein they pasted materials, such as newspaper, cards and wallpaper, flatly on canvas. It reflected a kind of liberation because the artist was free to compose or invent patterns and spatial qualities.

Papier Decoupé (Paper Cutout)

A form of "drawing" with scissors by Matisse (1869–1954) whereby he created optical illusions with bands of colors and colored forms. He said, "Cutting to the quick in color reminds me of the sculptor's direct carving."

Papier-Māché

Strong but light molding paper pulped with glue and other substances.

Parergon

A glimpse of a detail (landscape, flowers, etc.) to give an added interest.

Paris, School of

From the mid-1800s to the onset of World War II, the world of art revolved around Paris. Many of the major movements or forces were formulated there. Its most well known artists include: Monticelli (1824–1886); Puvis de Chavannes (1824–1898); Boudin (1824–1898); C. Pissarro (1830–1903); Manet (1832–1883); Degas (1834–1917); Fantin-Latour (1836–1904); Legros (1837–1911); Sisley (1839–1899); Cezanne (1839–1906); Redon (1840–1916); Monet (1840–1926); Morisot (1841–1895); Renoir (1841–1919); H. Rousseau (1844–1910); Gauguin (1848–1903); van Gogh (1853–1890); Bonnard (1867–1947); Vuillard (1868–1940); Matisse (1869–1954); Denis (1870–1943); Roualt (1871–1958); Villon (1875–1963); Vlamnick (1876–1958); R. Dufy (1877–1953); Leger (1881–1955); Picasso (1881–1973); Braque (1882–1963); Modigliani (1884–1920); La Fresnaye (1885–1925); Soutine (1894–1943).

Pastel Chalk a/k/a French Pastels

Made by mixing ground pigment with water and a binder to produce stiff paste, and so on. This dry crayon is considered a painting medium because its substance can be spread. Other dry mediums are basically used in drawings.

Pastiche

The imitation of another artist's work; deceptive art.

Pastoral

A rural picture or scene.

Patina

A surface appearance of something grown beautiful over the years.

Patroon Painters (1675–1750)

The first American school. The artists were influenced by English and Dutch styles and painted in a linear and flat style. Even though there was much originality in their Naive Art, they used mezzotints as models.

Pattern

1. A repeated motif.
2. A decorative, harmonious or symbolic design.
3. A design created through the interplay and contrast of colors.

Pattern and Decoration a/k/a P&D or The New Decorativeness (1970s)

The artists used cheap fabric, old furniture, etc. as part of their observation of world poverty and in their representations of funky eclecticism. Kozloff (b. 1942); MacConnel (b. 1946); Smyth (b. 1948); Kuschner (b. 1949); among others.

Pattern Book

1. A medieval book which contained general forms for the human figure for use by painters and sculptors.
2. A book of motifs and designs used for reference by artists and industrial designers.

Peale Family, The

Its patriarch, Charles W. (1741–1827) sired 17 children, many of whom were outstanding artists, including Raphael (1774–1825), Rembrandt (1778–1860), Rubens (1784–1864) and Titian (1799–1885), who were named after master artists. Charles' brother, James (1749–1831), another talented artist, was the father of Sarah (1800–1885). Aside from art, family members possessed diverse talents. They are considered the first family of Early American art.

Pentimenti

1. The alterations made by an artist in the process of painting.
2. The re-appearance of drawings beneath the surface because of the aging of the canvas, particularly if there are layers of glaze.

Penumbra

A shaded area between perfect shadow and full light.

Percent for Art—See Public Art.

Perception

An impression of a subject obtained by the senses.

Performance Art a/k/a Body Art (1960s–1980s)

It has been called "the most immediate form . . . getting down to the bare bones of . . . communication: art/self and confronting audience/society." Any subject, medium or material is presented by the Performance artist at any time, anywhere and for any duration, in direct communication with an audience. In 1977 when 54 avant-guarde artists presented Happenings and Performance Art, the Performances were categorized into several themes: the body, the senses, music, the spoken word, identity and society. Another Performance was documented by diagrams, photographs and interviews with artists. This art form continues to flourish. Beuys (1921–1986); Paik (b. 1932); Acconci (b. 1940); Gilbert and George (both b. 1942); among others. See **Happenings.**

Perspective

A technique invented during the Early Renaissance which applied a quasi-mathematical system to the portrayal of three dimensionality on a two-dimensional surface. Essentially, it is a system where the illusion of reality is obtained. Several well known types of perspective are:

—Foreshortening	The shortening of a single unit, such as an arm or a leg. This type was used in Egyptian and Greek art before the laws of perspective were fully understood.

—Descriptive	An arrangement of figures according to importance of rank, a form used in ancient times.
—Aerial a/k/a Atmospheric	The use of color and tone; the far scene is paler in color or grayish.
—Linear	The use of converging lines.
—Skiagraphy	The correct gradations of light and shade in order to project shadows.
—Oblique	To render an object turned at an angle.
—One point	A human figure near the vanishing point appears farther and smaller than a figure in the foreground.
—Reverse	It allows multiple points of view in one painting; figures also appear the same size anywhere in the painting.

With his essays on form, shape, depth and light, Piero della Francesca (1416–1492) is credited with developing theories of perspective. Brunelleschi (1377–1446), an architect, whose work established a pattern for architecture for the ensuing 500 years, discovered linear perspective. This naturalistic effect became the basic element of European painting for the next five centuries. Masaccio's (1401–1428) "The Holy Trinity" is one of the first paintings made following the theories of perspective. See **Space**.

Petard

A work of art created to attract attention because of its strange color, composition or theme.

Petroglyph

An ancient form of engraving images on stones.

Photomontage

A kind of collage, consisting of photographically reproduced images from newspapers and magazines which are applied to the support to give the effect of film editing. This technique was used largely for propaganda purposes and social criticism. Hausmann (1886–1971); Heartfield (1891–1968); Grosz (1893–1959); among others. It was developed into a Surreal technique by Ernst (1891–1976).

Photomural
A very large photographically produced mural applied to a interior surface. See **Supergraphics.**

Photo-Realism (1960s–1970s)
It has been referred to by several titles, but it has no special identity other than Realism: photographs are seemingly copied in clinical detail. Goings (b. 1928); Bailey (b. 1930); Flack (b. 1931); Morley (b. 1931); Cottingham (b. 1935); Estes (b. 1936); Kleeman (b. 1937); Eddy (b. 1944); among others. See **Super Realism.**

Photo-Secession (1902–1910)
An association of American photographers formed by Stieglitz (1864–1946) in order to gain recognition of photography as a fine art. Steichen (1879–1973) was a founding member.

Pictographs
The art of picture writing of pre-historic and ancient times. Several Abstract Expressionist painters were inspired and influenced by Native American art, which resulted in paintings called "pictographs." Gottlieb (1903–1974); Pollock (1912–1956); among others.

Pictorial Arts
Includes painting, drawing, photography and the Graphic Arts.

Picture Plane
The plane occupied by the surface of the picture.

Picturesque
Referring to the charming elements of a scene.

Pigment
A color derived from a powdered form obtained from the earth, stones, minerals, animals, vegetables or chemicals and bound together with an adhesive such as egg, oil, glue or other substance.

Plane
A flat or level surface; a single dimension.

Plastic Art

A visual art as opposed to written art, usually related to sculpture.

Plasticity

1. The quality of three dimensionality in a plastic medium (pottery, sculpture, etc.)
2. The semblance of three dimensionality attained with the use of light, shadow and content.
3. The sense of form achieved through the molding of materials.

Plein Air

Referring to the painting of pictures out-of-doors to impart the quality of open air.

Pointillism—See Neo-Impressionism.

Polychrome Sculpture

Much ancient sculpture as well as that of medieval and Renaissance years was multicolored in an attempt to make it more life-like.

Polymorphic

The appearance of a work of art seems to change according to the viewer's position. See **Kineticism.**

Polyptych

A work of art consisting of three or more parts.

Pont-Aven Group

A group of artists who worked in Brittany under the charismatic leadership of Gauguin (1848–1903). They were preoccupied with the theory and practice of art. Mayer de Haan (1852–1895); O'Conor (1860–1940); Laval (1862–1894); Serusier (1863–1927); Bevan (1865–1925); Forbes-Robertson (1865–1935); Bernard (1868–1941); among others. See **Cloisonnism** and **Synthetism.**

Pop Art (1960s–1970s)

The impetus for this movement developed from discussions between English critics, sculptors, architects and painters in the mid-1950s, who were interested in the new urban culture, especially as manifested in the U.S. Its English adherents were Tilson (b. 1928); Blake (b. 1932); Hockney (b. 1937); Jones (b. 1937); Phillips (b. 1939); among others. Pop Art was promoted by dealers and adopted in the U.S. with extraordinary speed.

Essentially, Pop had a dual quality: parody and the conversion of ordinary objects into "icons" when presented out of context. Appropriated images and artifacts from everyday life, the media and traditional painting were fused with the techniques, colors and scale of advertising art. This anti-high art resulted in a sophisticated instant "culture."

Even though Pop artists shared the same viewpoint, each developed a unique style or image. Lindner (1901–1971); Thiebaud (b. 1920); Hamilton (b. 1922); Rivers (b. 1923); Lichtenstein (b. 1923); Segal (b. 1924); Rauschenberg (b. 1925); Warhol (1928–1987); Oldenburg (b. 1929); Johns (b. 1930); Wesselmann (b. 1931);Rosenquist (b. 1933); Ramos (b. 1935); Goode (b. 1937); Ruscha (b. 1937); among others.

In Germany known Pop artists include Richter (b. 1932); Vostell (b. 1932); Nofer (b. 1937); Klapheck (b. 1938); among others.

Portfolio

1. A container for drawings or prints.
2. The artist's collection of works on paper.
3. In Commercial art, a collection of the artist's work to be shown as a sample for sale or exhibition.

Portfolio Edition

A series of prints depicting one theme. The portfolio can be rendered by one artist or a group of artists. The prints may be sold separately or as a unit.

Portraiture

A painting, sculpture, drawing or other representation of a person, living or dead; the capture of the essence of a person's facial features. That essence, however, is open to interpretation by the artist. Portraiture is an art form that has been practiced since Egypt, but it was not until after 1400 that depicting likenesses became a regular art form in Europe. Among hundreds of portraitists, those who excelled are:

European—van der Weyden (1400–1464); Clouet (1486–1540); Titian (1490–1576); Holbein (1497–1543); Tintoretto

(1518–1594); Hals (1580–1666); Velasquez (1599–1660); Rembrandt (1606–1669).

English—van Dyck (1599–1641); Reynolds (1723–1792); Cotes (1726–1770); Gainsborough (1727–1788); Wright (1734–1797); Beechey (1753–1839); Hoppner (1758–1810); Lawrence (1769–1830); Watts (1817–1904); John (1878–1961).

American—Copley (1737–1815); Earl (1751–1801); Stuart (1755–1828); Trumbull (1756–1843); Rembrandt Peale (1778–1860); Sully (1783–1872); Sarah Peale (1800–1885); Bingham (1811–1879); Elliott (1812–1868); Eakins (1844–1916); Sargent (1856–1925); Henri (1865–1929); Rand (1876–1941); Kuhn (1880–1949); Speicher (1883–1962); Neel (1900–1984); A. Wyeth (b. 1917); Bachardy (b. 1934). See **Faiyum Portraits, Limners** and **Nude Art.**

Poster

A decorative bill for posting in public; an artistic rendition of an advertisement; a low cost reproduction of a painting. The essentials of Poster Art are clarity, simplicity and timely or humorous theme. Toulouse-Lautrec (1864–1891) invented Poster Art as it is known today. Several artists who excelled were Penfield (1866–1925), Bonnard (1867–1947), Sloan (1871–1951), Beardsley (1872–1898) and Shahn (1898–1969), among others. Recognizing that art was a powerful tool in the dissemination of ideas, posters became a primary form for the creation of agitation and propaganda in the Soviet Union and other revolutionary areas.

Post-Impressionists (1880s-early 1900s)

A term describing several artists or movements who used Impressionism as their starting point; they too believed that painting should be based on observation of nature. Artists recognized as highly individual representatives of Post-Impressionism include Cezanne (1839–1906) whose intention was to paint the reality lying beneath the surface of the subject and to emphasize its form and structure, and van Gogh (1853–1890) and Gauguin (1848–1903) who were influential in their use of striking color, lack of symmetry and ability to express themselves from their inner souls. Color was their language. Their theories and experiments led to Expressionism. See **Intimist Painters, Nabis** and **Fauvism.**

Post-Minimalism (1960s)

A seemingly subverted art form with the suggestion of comedy, eccentricity or mystery. Hesse (1936–1970) executed a "painting" made with rubber washers; Kosuth (b. 1945) used enlarged photostats to define words which he called the "art as idea as idea" series.

Postmodernism

A reaction to Modernism, sometimes called antimodernism, and an attempt to maintain the traditional role of art as a renewal to the spirit of understanding.

Post-Painterly Abstraction (1960s)

It can embrace several styles or movements, such as Minimalism or Color Field painting. Its essential characteristics are flatness, linear clarity and broad color. The artists used color as both form and content. Albers (1888–1976); Glarner (1899–1972); Diller (1906–1965); Feeley (1910–1966); Louis (1912–1962); Noland (b. 1924); Youngerman (1926–1962); Held (b. 1928); Stella (b. 1936); Poons (b. 1937); among others.

Poussinism

The work of Poussin (1594–1665) was considered a model by 17th century academic painters who thought that the classical ingredients of drawing and design were fundamental and that color was only secondary. See **Rubenism.**

Precisionism—See Cubist Realism.

Pre-Columbian Art

The art of North, Central and South America from the period before the arrival of Columbus in America.

Pre-Historic Art—See Cave Art and Primitive Art.

Pre-Raphaelism (1848–1854)

An esoteric reform movement in England in reaction to Realism and Academy art. The artists wanted to depict the beauty of nature in outdoor painting and humankind in better proportions with simpler forms and the use of luminous colors. They were Realists, nevertheless, because they painted in precise detail. The key to their philosophy can be found in the writings of John

Ruskin: true to nature and moral feeling. These artists were influenced by the work of Fra Angelico and Lochner; they wanted to return to the art of the 1300s. Paintings were signed P.R.B. (Pre-Raphaelite Brotherhood). Hunt (1827–1910); Rossetti (1828–1882); Millais (1829–1896); Burne-Jones (1833–1898); among others. Their "spiritual father" was Ford (1821–1893).

Primary Structures (sometimes referred to as Minimal Structures)

Sculptures of steel and concrete which enabled the spectator to walk around or through. In 1952/1953 a temporary museum (The Echo) was established in Mexico City by Goeritz (b. 1915), a constructivist sculptor, to house these gigantic geometric sculptures. His ideas soon became international. D. Smith (1906–1965); Rosati (1912–1988); Bladen (b. 1918); Pepper (b. 1925); Judd (b. 1928); DiSuvero (b. 1933); King (b. 1934); DeMaria (b. 1935); Serra (b. 1939); among others.

Priming

To prepare a surface for painting by giving it a ground.

Primitive

Natural; self-taught; simple; austere; rudimentary

Primitive Art

The art of an early period of a culture. In the context of surviving primitive societies of the New Stone Age (Africa, the Americas and Oceania), it was concerned with the invisible world. In those societies, sculpture and art were intended for use in healing rituals, in magic, in ancestor worship and in connection with the underworld. Their seemingly distorted representations resulted from the belief that a living force came from God and filled the universe and all form. In essence, almost everything used in daily life was turned into a ritual art object to increase its efficiency or protective powers. Secular art did not exist and beauty was not a factor.

The role of carving was integral to daily life and important carvers were recognized as Masters, equal to chiefs or other village heads.

In the early part of the 20th century, art from Africa played an influential role in the work of Picasso, Modigliani and others. And it was only after the publication of "Primitivism in Modern

Art" in 1938 that African, Oceanic and Pre-Columbian art was considered serious art by historians.

The tradition of Primitive Art continues in Africa, but modern-day artists are not influenced by religion alone; symbolism and design have also become important motifs.

Primitives

A term applied to painters before 1450, especially in Italy and in the Netherlands.

Primitivism (1905–1920)

The Russian form of expression which evolved from Cubism and Futurism. The artists used simple, block-like forms and strong colors. Gontcharova (1881–1962); Larionov (1881–1964); Burljuk (1886–1917); among others.

Print

A reproduction of an original work of art. See Graphic Arts.

Printmaking

The design and production of prints. The original work is re-created through a Graphic Art process. The artist supervises the printing of the work in limited or multiple editions and thereafter the plate is usually scored or defaced. See Limited Edition and Multiples.

Process Art (1960s–1970s)

An art that grows during the period of creation. Its main criterion is perishability. Diverse raw materials (ice, grass, liquid, sawdust, etc.) are used and sited at random without structure and left to natural forces. The act of doing this is allegedly the art rather than the end product. It seems to make a statement for life itself. Gilliam (b. 1933); Dine (b. 1935); Hesse (1936–1970); Kounellis (b. 1936); Benglis (b. 1941); among others. See Conceptual Art.

Projection—See Three Dimensional.

Proletarian Art—See Socialist Realism.

Proof

An impression taken from a Graphic Art process. See Artist's Proof.

Proportion

The application of rules which regulate the relationship of parts to the whole, usually used in depiction of the human figure. See **Scheme** and **Scale**.

Proto

First in time; the beginning.

Prototype

The designation of an original creation.

Prouns (1920s)

An acronym in Russian for "Project for the Affirmation of the New" coined by Lizzitsky (1890–1941) for his paintings which appear to be plans for imaginary cities. Geometric forms (the circle and the sphere, the square and the cube, the triangle and the pryramid) were used during this period of experimentation. Also, the creation of constructions which seem to be floating in space.

Provenance

The history of ownership of a work of art and a guarantee of its authenticity.

Pseudomachines

The artistic mechanisms created by Tinguely (b. 1925). They groan and vibrate, but have no function. Some of his machines, however, produce Abstract Expressionist drawings. Also, the work of Greenblatt (b. 1960) whose colorful constructions of whimsical, cartoon-like figures, furniture and gadgets seem to capture the essence of childhood. He describes his work as "happy decorative art." Several titles: "Here We Go," "Treasure Ox," "The Boat." See **Audiokinetic Sculpture**.

Public Art

"Percent for Art" programs have been instituted by many city, county and state governments in the U.S. and in other countries. Essentially, a certain percentage of any budget allotted for new public buildings is devoted to the installation of art, but always with the view that the art will suit the site for which it is intended. The choice of artist is made through the process of viewing slides of the work of many artists. The final decision is rendered by a panel of experts from the art world along with the participation of concerned public officials.

Public Building Administration (formerly Section of Painting and Sculpture of the Treasury Department) (1934).

This agency was created for the purpose of adorning public buildings. Artists were paid only if the work was accepted. See **Federal Art Project.**

Public Works Art (1933–1934)

An agency created during the Great Depression to help poverty-stricken artists. It employed over 4,000 artists who produced 15,000 works. See **Federal Art Project.**

Purism (1918–1932)

A kind of machine art established in Paris. Its founders, Ozenfant (1886–1966) and Le Corbusier (1887–1965), campaigned "for the reconstitution of a healthy art" reflecting the spirit of the age. They favored the adaptation of form to function; emotion and expression were excluded. They wrote the manifesto "After Cubism" (1918) in which they called on artists to use unmixed colors and to use simple geometric forms. See **Suprematism** and **DeStijl.**

Puteau Group (1911–1913)

A discussion group led by Villon (1875–1963) and his brothers Duchamp (1887–1968) and Duchamp-Villon (1876–1918) to redefine the language of Cubism as practiced by Picasso and Braque. They criticized Analytical Cubism because it lacked human interest. Aside from the resolution of philosophical matters, new color harmonies were deduced and the aspects of modern day life, notably the machine, were brought into focus. (Their increased use of color led to the establishment of Orphism.) Villon's "The Little Machine Shop" (1946) is classic of these new principles. See **Bateau-Lavoir Group.**

Quadro Riportado

A term describing easel pictures seen in normal perspective. These are inserted as ceiling decorations.

Quattrocento

Designating the 400s (1400s) during the Renaissance, an age when many artists strived to imitate nature and when perspective was perfected.

Rayogram/Rayograph a/k/a Photogram

A print made from film that was exposed to light without the use of a lens. Man Ray (1890–1976)

Rayonism (1911–1914)

A Russian adaptation to European avant-garde movements. Its manifesto stated that "Rayonism is the synthesis of Cubism, Futurism and Orphism." It was concerned with dissolving form into rays of light. In some instances, pure abstraction resulted. Gontcharova (1881–1962); Larionov (1881–1964); among others.

Ready-Mades

A term coined by Duchamp (1887–1967) to describe pre-existing elements as "works of art" which, in reality, were objects taken from everyday life. Their newness was reflected by new placement. Duchamp used these ready-mades as an attack on traditional art. He changed forever the meaning of contemporary art. See **Dada**, **Assemblage**, and **Pop Art**.

Realism

To represent the external world in an objective and factual manner. The philosophy of Comte, called Positivism, taught that only things that can be seen and heard are real; therefore, the artist was obliged to describe objects of nature in accurate detail and not to create anything from his imagination. In 1846 the poet Baudelaire called for art that was expressive of "the heroism of modern life." Courbet (1819–1877) responded to that call when he turned away from the symbolic, literary and historical themes of European art that had lasted more than 1,000 years. His one-man show "Le Realisme" marked another revolution—when nature and contemporary life became the artist's models. Only that which existed was important: portraiture, landscape, contemporary society. Man and his problems became the central theme.

Recession

In art, recession gives the illusion of depth obtained through linear or aerial perspective.

Regionalism (1930s)

A movement based on art linked to the spirit of a place. It was derived from the desire to establish a genuinely American art by depicting American subject matter and to extol small-town

America. It basic doctrine was that an artist should paint what he knows best: his home territory. Wood (1892–1942) and other recognized Regionalists promoted competitions among painters of each region in the U.S. Their goal, however, was not realized. See **Western and Indian Art** and **American Scene Painting.**

Regional Schools

The expansion of regional schools in the U.S. in the 1960s and 1970s developed through the policy of the National Endowment for the Arts which dispersed funds to state and local organizations.

Regulating Lines

Geometric forms and proportions which are used as a "visual language" in painting.

Relief

An art half-way between painting and sculpture. Its techniques include:

Shallow	Built up area of impasto or other medium.
Bas or low	Cameo wherein the background is cut away or Intaglio wherein the design is below the surface.
Demi or half-relief	The dimensions of depth are roughly half that of low and high relief.
High	A sculpture from which at least half of the surface projects.

Remarque

In the Graphic Arts, a mark or sketch engraved on the margin of a proof, print or plate to indicate the particular stage reached.

Renaissance (1400s–1500s)

It was the first period in history to be aware of itself and to give itself a name. Essentially, it was a period of the rebirth of knowledge and culture in Europe, especially in Italy, under the aegis of classical literature and art. It was an age of discovery in perspective, knowledge of anatomy and knowledge of the classical form in architecture by the Italian masters. The rules of art criticism also developed whereby the criteria of good and bad art were modeled on classical tradition.

Art, on the whole, was Christian in its roots and its meaning, and "true moral philosophy" was required of its artists. Proto-Renaissance art during the Gothic period was represented by the work of Giotto (1266–1336) and Duccio (1260–1319). The work of Pisanello (1397–1455), Uccello (1397–1475), Botticelli (1444–1510) and Giorgione (1478–1510) was representative of the secular, humanist element of the Renaissance: these artists depicted scenes from history and legends. Florence was the seat of the Renaissance shortly after 1400. See **Early Renaissance** and **Humanism**.

Renaissance Man

A term of esteem given to a person who is expert and multi-talented in several areas, especially in intellectual activity and in the arts. Leonardo da Vinci is considered the embodiment of the Renaissance man.

Rendering

1. To represent an object.
2. To reproduce or represent by artistic means.

Replica

See **Copy**.

Repoussoir

1. A compositional device such as a figure or object placed in the foreground so that all other details are seen beyond it.
2. The use of dull colors around bright colors, etc. so as to achieve the illusion of depth.

Representational Art

The reproduction of a recognizable subject according to its physical appearance, as it is seen, in contrast to nonobjective or **Abstract Art**.

Reproduction

Any process or medium, usually print, that permits multiple copies of a work of art to be made.

Revolutionary Art

Reflecting the epic, heroic life of modern times. Goya (1746–1828); David (1748–1825); Delacroix (1798–1863); Daumier (1808–1879). In Mexico the work of Orozco (1883–1949) and Rivera (1886–1957) resulted in a multitude of murals depicting modern production, social criticism and revolution. See War Paintings.

Rhythm

1. Marked by regular repetition or natural flow.
2. Repeated shapes, patterns or colors.

Rococo (1730–1780)

A refined outgrowth of and a reaction to Baroque; it made its first appearance in France. Rococo was above all a style of interior decoration. In art it was a decorative style marked by curving line, soft contour, soft light and bright colors. In France, two styles evolved:

1. Striking colors, decorative motif, sensual or frivolous subjects. Boucher (1703–1770); Fragonard (1732–1806).
2. Genre scenes depicting in exaggerated form the value of domestic virtues. Chardin (1699–1779); Greuze (1725–1805).

In England, Rococo had the effect of bringing about the first important school of English painting in decades. Hogarth (1697–1764); Wilson (1714–1782); Reynolds (1723–1792); Gainsborough (1727–1788).

In Italy, Rococo was represented by the work of Venetian artists Tiepolo (1696–1770); Canaletto (1697–1768); Longhi (1702–1785); Guardi (1712–1793).

Porcelain figures made under the hand of Bustelli (1723–1763) in France are classic of Rococo sculpture. The carved wooden statues of Gunther (1725–1775) are classic of German Rococo. See Neoclassicism.

Roman (Empire) Art

The Greco-Roman period (145 B.C.–400 A.D.) was actually an extension of the Classical period of Greece. Under Augustus, Greek ideas in art and architecture spread throughout the Empire. The Empire's most significant contribution, nevertheless, was that of architecture, including town-planning and the creation and adornment of interiors. In the latter category, the Pantheon in Rome and the Temple of Bacchus in Lebanon are classic, among others. The three principle achievements of art in the Roman world were the development of portraiture, narrative and landscape. Known art forms were sculpture, narrative relief, fresco painting and portrait busts. The best examples of Roman art are those found in Pompei (1st century B.C.). There was also a great concern with ancestors for whom wax masks were made. In the crafts, there were many well known silversmiths. See **Early Christian Art.**

Romanesque (950–1150)

Since it was the age of the Crusades, and more knowledge of Byzantium was available, the ideals of Eastern art dominated. Manuscript illumination remained the traditional art form, but stronger colors were used. Tapestries, mosaics, wall paintings and stained glass were other major art forms. This period of culture was very productive of impressive sculpture and the erection of churches, most notably the cathedral of Bamberg in Germany and the church of Santiago de Compostella in Spain. Romanesque sculpture has been called "the first step . . . in representational art." See **Ottonian Renaissance** and **Gothic.**

Romanists

Flemish artists of the 1500s who were drawn to and influenced by the arts and antiquities of Rome.

Romanticism (1790s–1830s)

A representational style that influenced art of the imagination, with literature leading the way. The artists triumphed in beauty, strange lands, passionate expression and strong colors. Delacroix (1798–1863) and Gericault (1792–1824) were leaders of Romanticism in their use of historical, religious and literary themes. Majestic landscape, in general, emerged as a favored art form, especially in England, Germany and the U.S. See **Barbizon School** and **Landscape.**

Rotorelief

A disc modeled on a phonograph record. When "played," the design would give the illusion of disappearing into itself. Duchamp (1887–1967); Man Ray (1890–1976).

Rubbings

The placing of tracing papers over brass plaques and rubbing them with a substance to obtain a direct impression. See **Frottage.**

Rubenesque

A description of figures painted by Rubens because of their fullness and their curves.

Rubenism

A school of thought in France in the 1600s that held that color was as important as design and that color was the essence of life and nature. See **Poussinism.**

Salon des Refuses (1863)

An exhibition set up by Emperor Napoleon III, considered a landmark, to display the work of artists who had been refused by the official academy.

Salon Painting

A style acceptable to the Paris Salon, according to academic tradition.

Scale

The comparison of the size of the painted subject to realistic size.

Scale Life

Life size, full-length portraits.

Scheme

The basic proportions for the drawing of objects to conform to appearance, based on the canons of proportion from ancient times and antiquity, but developed into a simplified schemata following Renaissance research.

School

1. Comprised of a geographical area (national, regional or local).
2. A following especially applicable to the Middle Ages when certain masters had their own shops or certain cities had their own groups of artists.
3. Artists working together who create an inventive atmosphere.
4. Commonality in the use of certain artistic techniques.

Scrimshaw

Articles made from whalebone and whale ivory on which incised lines were filled with pigment in a decorative style. It was a popular craft in the 1800s.

Sculptopeinture

A title given by Archipenko (1887–1964) to his paintings wherein forms which appear to be in relief are actually flat, while others are built up from carved plaster. He was able to manipulate his own solids and voids, all in accordance with the spirit of Cubism.

Sculpto-Pictoramas

An art form peculiar to Grooms (b. 1937) wherein entire rooms are filled with constructions of humorous or satirical replicas of buildings, bridges, public transportation, etc., including caricatures of known personalities and characters. The viewer is confronted with a fun-filled environment of images that seem to be continually happening through the use of sound or moving parts. Titles of these fields of action include "City of Chicago," "Ruckus Manhattan" and "Ruckus Rodeo." See Pseudo-machines.

Sculpture

Its three major forms include:

1. Carved (cutting up).
2. Modeled (building up).
3. Assembled (the joining or construction of prefabricated elements).

Its three dimensionality creates volume, mass and presence in space. Common materials include wood, marble, stone, bronze, clay, fiberglass, plaster, wire. Among its masters: Quercia (1375–1438); Donatello (1386–1466); Michelangelo (1475–1564); Cellini (1500–1571), Bernini (1598–1680); Rodin (1840–1917), the "father" of modern sculpture; Renoir (1841–1919); Pompson (1855–1923); Rosso (1858–1928);Brancusi (1876–1957); Young (1877–1957); Storrs (1885–1956); Robus (1885–1964); Manship (1885–1966); Archipenko (1887–1964); Lipchitz (1891–1973); Moore (1898–1986); Savage (1900–1962); Nevelson (1899–1988); Giacometti (1901–1966); Dubuffet (1901–1985); Hepworth (1903–1975); David Smith (1906–1965); Manzu (b. 1908); Bourgeois (b. 1911); T. Smith (1912–1980); Sugarman (b. 1912); Pavia (b. 1912); Caro (b. 1924); Jackson (b. 1924); J. S. Johnson (b. 1930); Marisol (b. 1930); Bontecou (b. 1931); Gallo (b. 1933); Frank (b. 1934); Graves (b. 1940); Kirili (b. 1940); DeAndrea (b. 1941). See Minimalism, Primary Structures and Computer Portrait Sculpture.

Sculptured Wall

An art form peculiar to Nevelson (1899–1988) who constructed reliefs from boxes and compartments filled with abstract assemblages and thereafter painted them gold, white or black. Her more recent constructions are created with a variety of materials, such as aluminum, steel, lucite, etc.

Scumbling

The dragging of opaque color over other painted colors for a softened tonal effect—the opposite of glazing.

Seascape Painting

A popular art form during the 1800s. The sea was the great unknown and as such man's respect and fear of it were expressed in action-filled pictures depicting historic or romantic shipwrecks, whaling expeditions, the effects of weather, etc. Among its masters: Buttersworth (1817–1894); Hamilton (1819–1878); Jongkind (1819–1891); Raleigh (1830–1925); Homer (1836–1910); Lever (1876–1958); Dougherty (1877–1947); Stearne (1878–1957); Hansen (1886-1957); Garin (b. 1925); among others. See **Marine Painting.**

Secession (Sezession) (1890s-early 1900s)

A term used by several groups in Austria and Germany who wanted to break away from Academy art and whose Expressionist art contained touches of elegance in comparison to harsh Expressionism. Perhaps the Vienna Secession (1897) is the most memorable of these groups because one of the founding members was Klimt (1862–1918). The decorative quality of Art Nouveau was an important influence on his work. Kokoschka (1886–1980); Schiele (1890–1918); among others.

Self-Portrait

A rendering of the artist's own likeness. Rembrandt (1606–1669) probably portrayed himself more than any other painter. His series of self-portraits constitutes an autobiography.

Serial Art (1960s)

An art form wherein work in several parts or with different versions of the same subject or with different materials are produced. In most cases, each part of the series is incomplete by itself; all the pieces together act upon one another. Feeley (1910–1966); LeWitt (b. 1928); Stella (b. 1936); Storey (b. 1948); among others. (Multiples are also referred to as a form of Serial Art.)

Sfumato

The blending of light and dark tones in order to create a soft, delicate effect. This technique is attributed to Leonardo da Vinci.

Shade
The absence of illumination in a picture indicated by a color or a tone. Refer to Color Vocabulary.

Shade Picture
A profile portrait usually cut out of shaded paper; a silhouette.

Shaped Canvas (1950s–1960s)
The extension of painting into the third dimension wherein easel painting takes on the appearance of a sculptured form because of the shape of the canvas. Newman (1905–1970); Hamilton (b. 1922); Kelly (b. 1923); Hinman (b. 1932); Williams (1934–1988); Stella (b. 1936).

Sheen
Bright, shining.

Shimmer
Subdued sparkle.

Ship Portraits—See Marine Painting.

Shop Tradition (Bottega)
A training center for artists in Italy during the Early Renaissance or Late Gothic years.

Sienese School
Duccio (1260–1319); P. Lorenzetti (1280–1348); Martini (1285–1344); A. Lorenzetti (active 1319–1348); Barna (active 1330–1360); Bartolo (1330–1410); DiBartolo (1370–1428); Domenico (1400–1447); DiPietro (1406–1481).

Signature Style
The repetitive use or representation by an artist of an image, color or contour or the use of a process or medium that helps the viewer to attribute the work.

Silhouette—See Shade Picture.

Silversmith
An artisan who makes and repairs articles of silver.

Simplified Form
Form is reduced to its basic essentials.

"Simplified" Impressionism
The practice of Dove (1880–1946) in transforming his subjects into broad areas of color with the use of an optical projector.

Simultaneous Representation
The portrayal in a picture of more than one view of a person or a subject.

Simulationism—See Neo-Geo.

Sinking In
The matte effect of an oil painting when pigment is absorbed by the ground.

Sinuous
Winding or twisting movement; complex.

Sistine Chapel Ceiling
A series of murals located in the Vatican, depicting Biblical stories and covering an area of over 10,000 square feet with 343 painted figures. This masterwork by Michelangelo has been described as the greatest art ever done by man and is considered a tribute to the beauty of man and his redemption. Michelangelo's abilities seemed to be divinely inspired and life enhancing; he was called "il divino." Master artists who painted wall frescoes in the chapel include Signorelli (1441–1523); Perugino (1446–1523); Raphael (1483–1520).

Site-Specific Art
Art or sculpture that is created specifically for a certain site in a designated area. See **Public Art** and **Mural**.

Sketch
An unstudied or spontaneous drawing or painting usually used as a draft for a finished painting or sculpture. Various types of sketches include abbozzo, color sketch, croquis, esquisse, pochade, note, and study.

Sketch Box

A small wooden or metal box used for carrying oil painting equipment, including palette, brushes, tubes, turpentine, etc.

Social Realism

The use of art to convey the artist's viewpoint on contemporary life as when Young (1866–1943) protested child labor and championed women's suffrage, racial equality, etc. Daumier (1808–1879); Dore (1832–1883); Biddle (1885–1973); Grosz (1893–1959); Marsh (1898–1954); Shahn (1898–1969); Evergood (1901–1973); Bell (1906–1970); Guttosa (1912–1987); Fougeron (b. 1912); J. Levine (b. 1915); Lawrence (b. 1917); Coe (b. 1951); among others. See **Ashcan School** and **14th Street School.**

Socialist Realism

Realistic painting with the contemporary life of the working class as its primary subject was widespread in many countries, especially in the Soviet Union which favored proletarian art. In 1932 the U.S.S.R. established the Union of Soviet Artists, simultaneously abolishing all other artistic groups. The same sequence of events occurred in Germany under the Nazis.

Soft-Edge or Soft-Focus Painting

Curved or gentle image; a tactile, caressing style conveying a suggestion of unity and fluency. See **Hard-Edge Painting** and **Painterly.**

Soft Forms

Loose brushwork, large strokes.

Soft Sculpture

The Pop Art of Oldenburg (b. 1929) is representative of this style. His specialty is stuffing canvas to create monumental, boldly-colored, humorous replicas of American-style staples and objects: popsicles, cream pies, hamburgers, etc. Sekimachi (b. 1926); Sonnier (b. 1941).

Solid Forms

Geometrical forms (cube/sphere) having three dimensions.

Solid Painting

Painting in oil with a loaded brush to build up with a thick impasto.

Sotto In Su

The extreme of illusion in foreshortening which shows figures painted on a ceiling that seem to be floating in space.

Space

In one, two or three dimensions, a limited extension in distance, area or volume. The simplest and oldest type of space is two dimensional which lacks perspective. Naturalistic or optical space relates to how things are perceived—a method perfected during the Early Renaissance as perspective. It remained the standard until Cezanne and those following him attempted to modify it.

Sporting Pictures and Prints

Pictures portraying sports and animals endemic to England. These styles flourished from the 1780s to the 1850s. Stubbs (1724–1806); Marshall (1767–1835); Herring (1795–1865); Hancock (1795–1868); Tait (1819–1905); among others. See **Wildlife and Natural History.**

Stabile

A term devised by Arp to describe the large abstract sculptures of Calder (1898–1976). They have no moving parts and give the appearance of being rooted in place.

Stain

To spread with color; to chemically affect material, such as wood or glass, with color.

Stained Glass

A craft originating in antiquity, which involves the use of small pieces of colored glass to create designs, patterns or stories; also, colored glass windows. The Gothic period was especially known for the beauty of its stained glass during the Age of Great Cathedrals. Renaissance artists and modern artists have designed stained glass windows.

Stain Painting a/k/a Color Painting or Color Field Painting (1950s–1960s)

A technique developed by Frankenthaler (b. 1928) which made possible a new kind of painting, without brushwork. She poured thin acrylic paint onto an unprimed, unstretched canvas that soaked into the canvas which was then folded; the colors would flow. Also, a term used in ceramics. Louis (1912–1962); Olitsky (b. 1922); Noland (b. 1924); Mehring (b. 1931); among others. See **Washington Color Painters.**

DeStijl (The Style) (1917–1931)

A movement formed in Holland by Mondrian (1872–1944) and van Doesburg (1883–1931) with the publication of the magazine "DeStijl." They hoped to develop "a new awareness of beauty." They wanted to help modern man become receptive to new developments in the arts with writings of the artists themselves. DeStijl embraced painting, architecture, furniture, the decorative arts and typography. It was a strong influence on Bauhaus architecture. The style practiced by Mondrian, along with van der Leck (1876–1958), Huszar (1884–1960) and van Doesburg, was called "Neo-Plasticism." These artists reduced their representations into nonobjective abstractions. Curved lines were considered too personal. Mondrian religiously thought he could change the condition of human life with his paintings. Glarner (1899–1972) was a pioneer of Neo-Plasticism in the U.S. after his migration in the 1930s. See **Bildarchitektur.**

Still-Life

An art form that can be traced to antiquity wherein a painting or drawing is contrived by the artist according to his interpretation of a certain theme. In rendering still-life, inanimate objects are posed at close view whereby the artist can study the interplay of light, form, color and texture. Still-life reached its fullest expression in 17th century Holland where it went through three basic stages: the first that was modest, perhaps showing bread and cheese on crockery; the second a little richer with fruit and pewterware; the third emphasized the luxurious life. Its Dutch masters include deHeem (1606–1684); van de Velde (1619–1663); Kalf (1619–1693); van Beyern (1620–1690) and van Aelst (1626–1683). Later masters include Chardin (1699–1779); Raphael Peale (1774–1825); J. Francis (1808–1886); Hall (1825–1913); Mary J. Peale (1827–1902); Wm. Brown (1828–1898); Cezanne (1839–1906); Harnett (1848–1892); van Gogh (1853–1890); Peto (1854–1907); Chapin (1859–1927); Peterson (1876–1965); Hartley (1877–1943); Morandi (1890–1964); Freilicher (b. 1925); Maury (b. 1935); Fish (b. 1938); J. Moore (b. 1946); Gordon (b. 1953). See **Trompe L'oeil.**

Stippled

A technique of applying color with the point of the brush in repetitive small touches of dots and flecks to create a gradation of light and shade.

Stock Art—See Clip Art.

Stroke—See Brushwork and Hand of the Artist.

Structure

The stressing of pieces together; a manner of construction. Also, a style peculiar to Snelson (b. 1927) who structured free-standing, monumental, light-weight sculptures using cables and aluminum tubing as his primary materials, all of which give the appearance of space art. See **Drawing in Space.**

Structurism

A term originating with Biederman (b. 1906) who reacted against Constructivism and began to create a new kind of construction which consisted of three-dimensional, monochromatic, geometric forms posed at right angles against a colored background. His earlier work consisted of three-dimensional reliefs which he called "constructionism" or "constructions after nature." As a result of the latter art form, he was internationally recognized as the theorist of the new art of Construction. In essence, it was a bridge connecting painting and sculpture.

Studio

An artist's workshop or painting room.

"Studio Of"

A work produced under the direction of the artist. See **Workshop Production.**

Style

1. A choice, either knowingly or unknowingly, by a person, school, group or cultural age within a geographical area, of a way of using certain components, such as color, form, composition, etc.
2. The mode of expression used.

Stylized

To represent according to convention rather than according to nature.

Subjective Painting

Art that originates with the inner feelings or the spontaneity of the artist and not in accordance with reality.

Suite

A common theme depicted in several paintings; a narrative form.

Supergraphics (1960s)

Monumental designs painted or applied to interior surfaces to give the illusion of widening space. It was a kind of optical art because of the distortion created: the architectural scale seemed changed. Solomon (b. 1932) was its pioneer.

Super Realism a/k/a Photo-Realism (1960s–1970s)

A figurative, almost photographic, style wherein the representation of the subject is caught at an expressive moment. In sculptural form, the quality of lifelikeness is its salient feature. The representation is so intense that the eye can see more than it would in real life. Hanson (b. 1925); Leslie (b. 1927); Morley(b. 1931); Estes (b. 1936); Salt (b. 1937); Close (b. 1940); DeAndrea (b. 1941); Davies (b. 1946); Jokinen (b. 1947); among others.

Support

Referring to the surface on which a painting is made, such as canvas, paper, wall, panel, etc.

Suprematism (1913/1915 et seq.)

An attitude of mind rather than an art movement, whereby Malevich (1878–1935) opined that works of art were suggestions of the subconscious mind. In his essays on Suprematism, Malevich stated that his new color realism should avoid any natural appearance or sensation, that it should not be expressive of any emotion except pure artistic feeling, and that it should be created from geometric forms. His nonobjective mystical representations were used as contemplative images to attain the "zaum" state—visions of "the non-existent revealed." See **Purism, Cubo-Futurism and Zaum.**

Surrealism (Going Beyond Reality)

A movement that gained recognition in 1924 and remained active until 1966 when the poet Andre Breton died; he was internationally recognized as the force behind Surrealism. It was part of Breton's blueprint to re-create humanism by liberating the mind of man. His ideas, however, evolved with each artist. The artists who were influenced by Freud's theories would re-create on canvas their own hidden reality in the form of a spontaneous release of imagery. The two major types of Surrealism were (a) distorted but recognizable figurative forms and (b) abstract fantasy. Essentially, ordinary things were taken out of context and made into something extraordinary. Techniques incorporated the use of found objects, composed objects, automatism, transformation, etc. Picasso (1881–1973); Arp (1887–1966); Savinio (1891–1952); Ernst (1891–1976); Miro (1893–1984); Masson (1896–1987); Delvaux (1897–1944); Sage (1898–1963); Magritte (1898–1967); Tanguy (1900–1955); Lam (b. 1900); Tanning (b. 1911); Matta (b. 1911); Esteban (b. 1914); among others.

Surreal Object

A progeny of Surreal painting that is represented in collage in three dimensions. It possesses no aesthetic value or use. The Object might suggest that reality obtained by interpretation of the mind. Breton called it "a convulsive beauty." Man Ray (1890–1976); Cornell (1903–1973); M. Oppenheim (b. 1913); among others.

Symbol

Any kind of shape, sign, form, pattern, color or line which is used by the artist to express abstract ideas or hidden meanings.

Symbolism (1890s)

The attempt to create a language by means of line and color; to paint not the object but the effect it produces. Essentially, a search for expressive form that could be universally understood. Levi, a writer on the occult, said, "Symbolism is the art of interpreting and evoking the conditions of the soul by means of colors and lines." G. Moreau (1826–1898); Redon (1840–1916); Gauguin (1848–1903); Hodler (1853–1918); Toorop (1858–1928); Klimt (1862–1918); among others. See Synthetism.

Synchromism (1913–1919)

The American counterpart of Orphism formulated by M. Russell (1886–1953) and MacDonald-Wright (1890–1973) before the recognition of Abstract Art. Geometric forms and vibrant harmony were their motifs. Instead of tonalism, they used light and dark colors as well as "strong" and "weak" colors to suggest depth. Hartley (1877–1943); Stella (1877–1946); Schamberg (1882–1918); among others.

Synthetism (1886–1891)

When Gauguin was in Brittany, he and his fellow artists, known as the Pont-Aven group or circle, were preoccupied with the theory and practice of art. They believed that line, form and color had their own meanings, whether or not used in recognizable images. Their primitive-like paintings were characterized by dark outlines, flat shapes, broad areas of color, rhythmic contours, and simple subject matter with allusion to dreams or visions. See Cloisonnism and Symbolism.

Tableau Objet
The concept developed by Picasso and Braque that a painting as built up or constructed had a separate life of its own in its independent attempt to re-create the external world. Essentially, the attempt to find a trompe l'esprit. See **Papier Collé**.

Tableau Vivant (living picture)
A scene is presented by silent participants.

Tachisme
The French term corresponding to Action Painting, whereby paint is applied in spots of color without theme. See **Art Informel**.

Tactile Values
Referring to the illusion of three dimensionality. See **Texture**.

Tapestries
Tapestries, made from heavy woven materials, were usually embellished with representations of real or mythical animals, flowers and other decorative subjects. They were also created to capture historical or momentous events, most notably during the long reign of Louis XIV of France. Their primary function, during the Middle Ages especially, was to cover bare walls and furniture.

Technique
1. A style in which an artist uses line and color, as a poet uses words.
2. The skill of an artist in the use of a medium as well as knowledge and mastery of the mechanics and the materials used.
3. The use of a certain process.

Tempera Painting
The application of pigment, mixed with egg yolk, egg white and/or other substance to panels coated with gesso.

Tempered
The mixture of elements in correct proportions.

Tenebrism—See **Chiaroscuro**.

Ten Ornaments of Nature

Leonardo da Vinci's theory of light, shade, color, body, figure, position, distance, nearness, movement and rest in the use of chiaroscuro, anatomy and perspective.

Ten, The

A group of American Impressionists who exhibited together in 1898 to protest Europeanism. They constituted a kind of academy and exhibited together annually for 20 years. The American approach to Impressionism was romantic and idealistic, and was especially suited to American landscape, as manifested by the Hudson River School in its last years. Monet was their greatest influence. Dewing (1851–1938); Weir (1852–1919); Simmons (1852–1931); Twachtman (1853–1902); Metcalf (1853–1925); De Camp (1855–1923); Hassam (1859–1935); Reid (1862–1929); Tarbell (1862–1938); Benson (1862–1951).

Ten, The

A group of artists committed to Modern Art.

Texture

Tactile values such as roughness or smoothness seem almost real. The technique of realistic detail depends, in the main, on the source of light in the picture.

Theme

A subject or topic of artistic representation.

Thin

Paint which is applied thinly—the opposite of impasto.

Three Dimensional

Possessing or seeming to possess the dimensions of width, height and depth whereby form and volume are perceived through gradations of tone.

Three-Dimensional Picture

A painting executed in relief with layers of materials.

Tonalism

The close arrangement or relationship of tones to create mood. See American Tonalism.

Tondo
A circular or round painting.

Topographical Art
The painting and drawing of specific places or objects, such as country houses, towns, etc. See Veduta.

Tradition
The rules of art that have passed from one generation of artists to the next. Its overuse can lead to convention or pastiche.

Trajan Column (A.D. 113)
This sculpture is located in the Roman Forum and is a classic example of the continuous style. It is considered the masterpiece of Roman historical art. The stone-cutting reveals a flow of action, going from episode to episode. Similar columns were created in other cities.

Transavantgarde Painting—See Bad Painting.

Transformation
In Surrealism the radical changing of subjects into different shapes or forms.

Translucent
Clear, transparent.

Translucid Painting a/k/a Golden Painting
Painting over a thin sheet metal or foil.

Transparency
The ability to transmit light.

Transparent Painting
The effect of watercolor or glaze is produced with the use of transparent pigments. See Wash.

Triptych
A painting in three parts.

Trompe L'oeil (deceives the eye)
Painted subjects are represented in almost photographic detail. This style is especially common to interior decoration.

Goodwin (1840–1910); Evans (1847–1898); Harnett (1848–1892); Pope (1849–1924); Haberle (1853–1933); Peto (1854–1907); Cope (1855–1929); Hirst (1855–1942); among others.

Twentieth Century Art

It is occasionally referred to as "Since Cezanne," who was the forerunner of Cubism and Abstract Art. He is regarded as the key to Modern Art.

Artists have always sought to change, to renew or to be influenced by other painters, but it is only in this century that art has changed so rapidly. The pace of development in other aspects of society, however, has been just as rapid. The first major change was the reversal of traditional ideas that art should portray beauty and the realities of the world. An important factor in turning away from representational painting was the advancement of photography. The artist felt that he had to find a newer, more original role. With the invention of new materials, the artist was able to explore new art forms.

291 Group

A group of American artists who exhibited at the photo studio operated by Stieglitz (1864–1946) in Manhattan. Stieglitz looked forward to new developments. He held about 80 showings in his studio to promote the work of American artists Marin, Dove, Demuth and O'Keefe, among others. He also introduced to America the work of Cezanne, Matisse, Braque, Picasso and others. When his studio closed in 1917, he continued exhibitions at two other galleries, namely, Intimate Gallery (1925–1929) and An American Place (1929–1946); both galleries promoted only American artists.

Umbrian School

Piero della Francesco (1416–1492); Bonfiglio (1420–1496); Da Forli (1438–1494); Antoniazzo (1440–1526); Raphael (1483–1520); Barocci (1535–1612).

Underground, The

A new term for modern artists, in line with avant-garde artists. The underground artist feels himself alienated and wants to set up a new society.

Underpainting or Underdrawing a/k/a Lay in or Macchia

The preliminary monochromatic layer of color beneath the overpainting or final coat, which plays an important part in the development of gradations and shadows.

Undertint—See Imprimitura.

Unit One (early 1930s)

A group of British artists whose only commonality was that they stood for the expression of a contemporary spirit in painting, sculpture and architecture.

Utrecht School

A group of Dutch painters who were in Rome for a decade (1610–1620) and who then worked together in Utrecht. Under the influence of Caravaggio (1569–1609) and Manfredi (1580–1620) they used religious and genre themes. In turn, they influenced other painters, such as Rembrandt, Hals and Vermeer, in the use of chiaroscuro.

Value

The relation of one part of a picture to another part with regard to lightness and darkness.

Vanishing Point

A point at which something disappears, an important element of linear perspective wherein parallel lines meet in order to obtain the illusion of depth and distance.

Vanitas

The use of objects in a painting as a reminder of the vanity of life or of the passing of life. See Memento Mori.

Variant—See Copy.

Varnish

A liquid transparent film applied to a painting to protect it and to give a certain gloss.

Veduta

A genre painting, drawing or print of a known place or town. See View Painting.

Vehicle

The liquid in which pigments are dispersed to make a paint. See Medium.

Veil

A thin transparent glazing of oil paint over a white ground.

Venetian School

Jacobello (1394–1439); J. Bellini(1400–1471); Ant. Vivarini (1415–1480); Gentile Bellini (1429–1507); Messina (1430–1479); B. Vivarani (1430–1491); Crivelli (1430–1495); Giovanni Bellini (1430–1516); Alv. Vivarini (1446–1505); DeRoberti (1456–1496); Carpaccio (1465–1526); Giorgione (1478–1510); Lotto (1480–1556); Titian (1490–1576); Bissolo (1492–1554); Tintoretto (1518–1594); Veronese (1528–1588); Balestra (1666–1740); Piazzetta (1638–1754); Tiepolo (1696–1770); Canaletto (1697–1768); Longhi (1702–1785); Guardi (1712–1793).

Verism

1. The concept in Modern Art that everyday subjects have their own worth, as opposed to romantic themes.
2. A disturbing reality associated with the New Objectivity movement.

Video Art (1960s–1980s)

Essentially, a new expressive art ritual using high tech as its vehicle in the creation of tapes of moving images of abstract or representational compositions, either with or without sound, often combined with assemblage, constructions, sculptural tableaux, performances, etc. Paik (b. 1932); Jonas (b. 1936); Schwartz (b. 1936); Kubota (b. 1937); Lucier (b. 1944); Barry (b. 1949); Royston (b. 1951); Viola (b. 1951); among others. See **Audio Installation Art**.

View Painting

A highly developed art in the 18th century in Italy wherein well-known tourist spots and famous ruins were realistically depicted, a chore now done by photographs. Panini (1691–1765); Canaletto (1697–1768); Guardi (1712–1793); Piranese (1720–1778); Bellotto (1720–1780); among others.

Vitruvian Figure

The allegation during the Renaissance that man's proportions are perfect because with his arms and legs extended he would fit perfectly into geometric forms, such as the circle or the square.

Volume

1. The representation of mass.
2. A measured, occupied space.
3. A three-dimensional quality, either solid or void.

Vorticism (1912–1915)

An advanced English movement formed by Lewis (1884–1957) as an outgrowth of Cubism and Futurism. Lewis stated that the aim of Vorticism was to "build up a visual language as abstract as music" using the "world of machinery" as a source. Its doctrine was that dynamic energy moved quickly through successive images into depth—a vortex. Atkinson (1873–1931); Dismorr (1885–1939); Nevinson (1889–1946); Wadsworth (1889–1949); Bomberg (1895–1957); Roberts (1895–1980); among others.

Wall Drawings

This novel technique was devised by LeWitt (b. 1928) whereby he rendered pencil drawings consisting of thousands of horizontal, vertical and diagonal lines on walls from which secondary patterns would emerge.

Wall Painting

A painting executed in any medium on a prepared wall.

Wanderers, The (1860s–1870s)

A group formed in Russia that broke away from Academy art in order to bring Socialist Realism to the people.

War Paintings

—Homer (1836–1910) depicted scenes from the Civil War in the U.S.

—X. R. Smith (1839–1929) painted battle scenes of the Civil War ("The Battle of the Monitor and the Merrimac" and "Rebel Rain Tennessee Attacking the U.S. Ships Richmond and Lackawanna").

—Sargent (1856–1925) painted in the battle area during World War I when he was 62 years old. Among his paintings were "The Arrival of American Troops at the Front, France, 1918" and "Gassed."

—Picasso (1881–1973) expressed his condemnation of the Spanish Civil War with "Guernica" (1937) and of the Korean War with "War and Peace."

—Stoops (1887–1948) As a soldier he made drawings of tired and grimy soldiers at the front during World War I.

—Pippin (1888–1946) painted the grim details of his war experiences in World War I. His most famous military painting is "The Ending of the War: Starting Home" (1931).

—P. Nash (1889–1946) executed drawings of the "landscape of war" at the front during World War I.

—Nevinson (1889–1946) recorded his wartime experiences (1916–1918) on canvas.

—Fautier (1898–1964) rendered "Otages," a series of paintings inspired by the horrors of war.

—Piper (b. 1903) painted pictures of bomb-devastated buildings during World War II.

—Guttuso (1912–1987) rendered "Wall Newspaper" as a condemnation of war.

—Golub (b. 1922) paints pictures of rioters, mercenaries, torturers and death-squad goons.

Wash

1. To paint thin color with a broad sweep of the brush.
2. The thin coating of paint.

Wash Drawing a/k/a Pen-and-Ink Drawing

A drawing executed with many dilutions of ink or monochromatic water color. It is often used in combination with other drawing media, such as charcoal, pencil or chalk. It is particularly effective in rendering light and shadow.

Washing Out

The removal of color from a watercolor.

Washington Color Painters (late 1950s–1960s)

The artists used staining and pouring techniques in large, abstract paintings. Louis (1912–1962); G. Davis (b. 1920); Noland (b. 1924); Downing (b. 1928); Mehring (b. 1931). See Stain Painting.

Washington Crossing the Delaware

A popular allegorical/historical painting by Leutze (1816–1868).

Watercolor

Pigment and water mixed with a binder, resulting in a clear or transparent color. Also, a work of art so produced.

The modern technique of transparent watercolor painting was developed by Girtin (1775–1802) and Turner (1775–1851).

Among its masters are English artists A. Cozens (1717–1786); J. R. Cozens (1752–1799); Cotman (1782–1842); Cox (1783–1859) and American artists LaFarge (1835–1910); Homer (1836–1910); Marin (1870–1953); McComas (1874–1938); and Whorf (1903–1959); among others.

Wax Paint

The pigment is mixed with bee's wax to create a substance used for impasto.

Wax Portraits

Portrait-making on wood panels following a naturalistic technique. This technique was common in Egyptian and Greek art.

Weaving

In modern times, it has become recognized as a unique American craft. The creation of a fabric is seen as a composition of colors and textures.

Western and Indian Art

Generally, the melding of Realism and Romanticism in the portrayal of the majesty of Western plains, mountains and canyons and in the pictorial history of cowboys, Indians, explorers, hunters, trappers, army expeditions, army posts, the railroad and frontier life. Among its masters: Catlin (1796–1872); Eastman (1808–1878); Miller (1810–1874); Bingham (1811–1879); Stanley (1814–1872); Deas (1818–1867); Raschen (1854–1937); Gaul (1855–1919); Cooper (1856–1924); Hauser (1859–1918); Sharp (1859–1953); Deming (1860–1942); Remington (1861–1909); C. M. Russell (1864–1926); D. C. Smith (1864–1939); Hudson (1865–1937); Couse (1866–1936); Leigh (1866–1955); B. Phillips (1868–1956); Sauerwein (1871–1910); Borein (1872–1945); F. T. Johnson (1874–1939); Schoonover (1877–1972); Gollings (1878–1932); Wieghorst (1899-1988); Pleissner (1905–1983); Lovell (b. 1909); Berke (b. 1921); F. McCarthy (b. 1924); Bama (b. 1926); Crowley (b. 1926); Terpning (b. 1927); Doolittle (b. 1947); Craven (b. 1950); M. McCarthy (b. 1951); Rohrig (b. 1955); among others.

Whirligig

An outdoor sculpture activated by the wind. In the 20th century, these movable parts are mass-produced in the form of windmills, flying ducks, and so forth.

White Writing

The technique of Tobey (1890–1976) whereby he covered his pictures with a network of marks in order to achieve harmony. Tobey believed that "painting should come from the avenues of meditation, rather than the canals of action."

Wildlife and Natural History

The creation of representational paintings that capture the spirit and the natural beauty of animals, fish, birds and the great outdoors. Among its masters: C. W. Peale (1741–1827); Wilson (1766–1813); Audubon (1785–1851); Titian Peale (1799–1885); Troye (1808–1874); Hinckley (1813–1896); Brackett (1823–1919); Bridges (1835–1923); Muir (1838–1941); Fuertes (1874–1927); Gromme (b. 1897); Adams (1922–1971); Shepherd (b. 1931); Ede (b. 1931); Hill (b. 1932); Daly (b. 1937); Combes (b. 1940); Doolittle (b. 1947); Miller (b. 1951); Marris (b. 1951); Daniel Smith (b. 1954); Frederick (b. 1956); Lyman (b. 1957); among others.

Wire Sculpture

The creation of form with wire and metal.

Wood Carving

The carving of wood to create relief sculptures or objects in the round.

Woodcut a/k/a/ Woodblock Print

A Graphic Art used in the production of prints, cards and books, especially when set up with movable type. Gauguin (1848–1903) revived its use in Modern Art, as did Picasso (1881–1973).

Work of Art

Referring to a painting or sculpture of high artistic quality.

Workshop Production a/k/a Shop Work

A work produced under the supervision of an artist, but usually manifesting less quality than original art.

World of Art (1890s)

A Russian movement embracing art, music and poetry. It promoted modern Western styles, especially Impressionism, in contrast to the aims of The Wanderers. They also espoused the doctrine "art for art's sake."

Worm's-Eye View

A scene depicted as though observed from below.

Zaum

A Cubo-Futurist language of the future that would convey knowledge "beyond the mind." Malevich (1878–1935) hoped that his paintings would serve as the visual expression of zaum perceptions. See Suprematism.

Zeitgeist

The spirit of the times.

Zero Group (1957–1966)

A group of German artists who were interested in kineticism and luminism. They wanted to explore the effects of color and light. Piene(b. 1928); Uecker (b. 1930); Mack (b. 1931); among others.

Color Vocabulary

Achromatic
Possessing no hue; a neutral; black, gray or white.

Advancing Colors
Any warm, strong or "hot" color which appears to come forward. See Warm Colors.

After-Image
If you stare at one color for about 30 seconds, and then look away at a white or grayish background, a different color will be seen. This is the complement of the color first viewed. When you look at red, you should get its complement of green, etc.

Analogous Colors—See Related Colors.

Atmospheric Color
Although an object may be locally colored, it is broken into hues, tints and reflections of other colors because of light and proximity. In essence, an object is perceived to be the color it seems to be at any given moment.

Biochrome
Of two colors.

Blazing Color
Brilliant color.

Body
The strength or covering power of a pigment.

Body Color
A term used to describe solid areas of color which are either scumbled or glazed.

Bright Color
A strong pigment with a touch of white.

Brilliant Color
Glittering; very bright.

Broad Color
Extending far and wide.

Broken Color
1. See **Optical Mixture.**
2. A color whose brilliance has been dulled or toned down by the addition of a complementary color.

Calm Color
Equality between warm and cool colors; equality between dark and light values.

Cast
1. Modification of color by adding a trace of hue.
2. A minute difference in color only visible on close examination.

Chroma
1. The quality of saturation or intensity.
2. The measurement of color content.

Chromatic
Relating to color sensations; highly colored; a broad range of clear, positive colors.

Close in Value
Colors in the same family; analogous colors. See **Related Colors.**

Color
Color is simply defined as the sensation produced in the eye by light rays (reflected light). The main dimensions of color are hue, intensity, tone and temperature. See **Spectrum** and **Factors of Color.**

Coloration
The use of colors; the state of being colored.

Coloring
The general impression of a work of art.

Colorist
An artist who is known for his use of colors.

Color Properties
A term used to evaluate the color characteristics of a pigment.

Color Scheme
The dominant colors used in a special setting, such as a picture or a room.

Color Variation—See Permanent Colors.

Color Wheel
A continuous range or sequence of colors resulting from the study of light by Isaac Newton. The twelve colors on the wheel consist of primary, secondary and tertiary values; all other colors are considered variations of these colors and hues. Primary colors are red, blue and yellow; secondary colors are emerald green, orange and violet; tertiary colors are red/orange, yellow/orange, yellow/green, blue/green, blue/violet and red/violet. See Secondary Colors.

Complementary Colors
Each primary color has a complementary color which is produced by mixing the other two primaries. The complementary color of red is green, a mixture of blue and yellow. The complementary color of blue is orange, a mixture of yellow and red. The complementary color of yellow is violet, a mixture of red and blue. Red and green are opposite to each other on the color wheel, as are blue and orange; yellow and violet. One complementary color completes and intensifies the other complementary color.

Confluent Colors
Areas of color that merge into one another.

Cool Colors
Derived from ice: blue, green and violet.

Dappled Color
Gray enlivened with patches of various colors.

Day-Glo Colors
A trade name for fluorescent colors; intense, daylight colors that have a glowing effect.

Dead Coloring
A monochromatic underpainting, a step in the process of oil painting.

Decorative Colors
They tend to be chosen for their restful and pleasing traits, as well as for their "in" style.

Deep Color
Highly saturated colors with low values.

Degraded Color
A color that has lost its liveliness because of the addition of a dulling or graying color.

Diffraction Colors
The colors produced when light passes through a surface.

Discolor
The change of color; fading or staining.

Dominant Color
The prevailing color or tone.

Earth Colors
Colors derived from metal oxides, such as yellow ochre, terra verte, umber and Venetian red.

Equal Tones
Various colors with the same brightness, darkness or other equal measurement.

Factors of Color
—Hue/tint
—Shade/intensity
—Effect of color in relation to other colors, atmosphere, distance and light.

Flesh Tints
Those colors used to reproduce the colors of the human body.

Fluorescent Colors
Bright and glowing colors.

Fugitive Colors
Pigments and dyes that fade.

Fundamental Colors
Primary or secondary colors.

Half-Tone
A shade of gray or a color whose value is half way between the darkest and lightest tone of that color.

Harmonizing Colors
1. Colors close to each other in warmth or coldness.
2. The same hue in different tints or shades.

Hue
1. The chromatic quality of a color.
2. A general word for the shade or tint of any color.
3. The color of anything identified by a common theme: a green is seen as bluish or yellowish; a brown is cool (greenish) or warm (reddish). It may also be designated by reference to a subject: cherry red.

Hue Harmony
The grouping of three analogous colors on the color wheel.

Intensity
The chroma or saturation of a color, as compared with colorless gray. The effect is brilliance or richness.

Intermediate Colors—See Tertiary Colors.

Iridescence
1. Glitter, a display of colors with a rainbow effect.
2. The color effect caused by the play of brilliant or spectrum colors which are called diffraction colors.

Kaleidoscope
An enlivened pattern of various colors.

Key
The characteristic color and tone of a painting. Light, bright colors are high key colors; dark tones are low key.

Lean Color
A color with very little oil.

Lightfastness
The ability of a color to resist exposure to daylight.

Local Color
The color of an object without consideration of the effect of light or atmosphere. The color usually attributed to a certain object: red apple, blue sky.

Longwave colors
Low energy colors that are not readily visible in diminishing light: red, orange, yellow.

Low Color
Weak or faint color.

Luminous Color
Bathed in light.

Modulating Color
The adjustment of one area of color to an adjacent color.

Monochromatic
A color that can be seen in its various hues, tints or shades. See **Related Colors**.

Monotint or Monotone
Having a uniform hue.

Mutations of Color
To undergo changes in color.

Muted Color
Toned down or softened with a bit of gray or brown pigment.

Neutral Colors
1. Colors which range from white to black, including off-whites and browns.
2. Nonassertive colors.
3. Neither warm nor cool.

Neutral Tones
Tones which act as a contrast to positive colors.

Noncolors
Black, white and gray.

Nonfigurative Color
The disregard of the known world in favor of the independence of color as an energetic force affecting the senses, a vital teaching in Modern Art.

Nuance
The fine distinction in shades and tints of colors.

Opaque
Not accessible to light.

Optical Mixture—Refer to main section.

Orchestration
1. An old Venetian method of color harmony.
2. The theory of harmony and contrast.

Overtone
Color reflecting light, as applied by the artist.

Palette
1. A particular range of colors in oil painting.
2. The assortment of colors used by an artist or by a school of painting. Refer to main section.

Parti-Colored
Showing different hues and shades.

Pastels
Soft colors produced by adding much white. Refer to main section.

Permanent Colors
Colors that resist the influence of other colors or the effect of atmospheric conditions. See Lightfastness.

Piebald
Various colors; dappled with black and white.

Pigment
1. A powdered substance that imparts color to other materials.
2. A substance used for coloring derived from different sources, such as the earth, stones, minerals, animals or vegetables. In modern times, many pigments are artificially produced.

Polychromatic
Showing a variety of colors.

Positive Colors
Primary and secondary colors.

Poster Colors a/k/a Show Card Colors
Inexpensive opaque colors made with a water soluble binder.

Primary Colors
The pure colors of red, blue and yellow which are the source for all other colors.

Prismatic Color
Highly colored; brilliant.

Progression
Progression from one color, or group of colors, to another.

Psychedelic Colors
Fluorescent; bright and glowing colors.

Pure Colors
1. A color that is not mixed with other colors.
2. Spectrum color.
3. Color that comes from the tube.

Purity of Color
The clarity of color according to its type.

Purity of Pigment
Freedom from impurities.

Radiant Color
Vividly bright; shining.

Rainbow Colors
The colors used by the Impressionists. See Spectrum.

Realistic Color
The exact, detailed color used to depict actual scenes from life, as opposed to Impressionist painting of atmospheric color.

Receding Color—See Cool Colors.

Reflected Color
1. A bright color which reflects on another surface.
2. A light that is reflected from a colored surface and tinged with that color.

Related Colors
Various shades of the same color (monochromatic) or colors adjacent to each other on the color wheel (analogous).

Retreating Colors
Cool colors that recede and suggest distance.

Rich color
Vivid; deep or dark colors.

Saturation—See Intensity.

Scrambled Colors
Oil colors that are lightly mixed on the palette with a brush, resulting in a lively effect rather than that which results from carefully blended colors.

Secondary Colors
The compounds of two primary colors producing a secondary color. The colors green, orange and violet are obtained by mixing primary colors: red and yellow equal secondary orange; red and blue equal secondary violet; yellow and blue equal secondary green. See Color Wheel and Spectrum.

Shade

1. The varying tones of any color of the spectrum produced by mixing the color with gray, black or white or with its complement.
2. A full degree of difference between two colors.

Shading

1. Gradation of tone.
2. Toning or filling in areas through shadows.
3. The absence of light.

Shadow

A color mixed with black.

Shortwave Colors

High energy colors that are readily visible in diminishing light: blue, green, purple.

Simultaneous Contrast

The way two colors act upon each other.

Solid Color

A single color or hue.

Spectrum

A beam of light through a glass prism results in bands of color resembling the colors of the rainbow: red, orange, yellow, blue/green, blue/violet and violet. White is produced by an equal mixture of these colors. Black is the absence of color.

Split Complement

A color and two hues on either side of its complement. Yellow is the complement of violet. The two hues analogous to violet are red/violet and blue/violet. Therefore, the split complement would be yellow, blue/violet and red/violet.

Striking Through

A color which assets itself when used in conjunction with other colors.

Surface Color

1. The color effect of a surface viewed by reflected light, as in Light On.
2. The color of the top layer of a painting.

Symbolic Colors

Certain colors have their own connotations, such as black for lack of innocence or mourning, white for joy or purity, red for energy and fervor, etc. Colors may have their own meanings in various countries.

Symbolist Colors

Sharply in opposition to reality. The painter expresses his feelings about the theme rather than what he sees.

Tarnish

To dull.

Temperature—See Cool Colors and Warm Colors.

Tertiary Colors

Colors which are made up of equal parts of primary and secondary colors. They are obtained by mixing primary color and its adjacent secondary color. See Color Wheel.

Tincture

A physical material that colors, dyes or stains.

Tinge

1. A color with a slight shade added.
2. A small modification of color.

Tint

The tones of a color which are produced by the addition of white.

Tonal Value

The arrangement of tones so that a relationship exists.

Tone

1. The degree of lightness or darkness reflected in tints or shades.
2. The quality of a color measured by value and saturation.

Tormented Color

In oil painting, a color that has been excessively worked—the opposite of freshness or brilliance.

Transparent Color

Sheer enough to be seen through.

Triadic Harmony

Three colors equally distant from each other on the color wheel—red, blue, and yellow or any other combination.

Undertone

1. The color effect when viewed by reflected light.
2. The characteristics of a color when it is diluted with white.

Value of Color

The value of a pigment is measured by light or brightness. In order to change a value, either black or white is mixed with the color to render its value light or dark. A darkish hue would be low in value; a light hue would be high in value.

Versicolors

Varied colors; changeable in color.

Vivid Colors

Strong; high chroma.

Warm Colors

Derived from fire and sunshine: red, orange and yellow.

White Light

Consisting of the spectrum of colors. If the color wheel is spun very fast, white will result. See Spectrum.

Bibliography

—Master Paintings from the Phillips Collection (Shorewood Fine Art Books, 1981)

—H. W. Janson, A Basic History of Art (Prentice-Hall, Inc., 1980)

—E. H. Gombrich, The Story of Art (Phaidon Press, 1978)

—N. Lynton, The Story of Modern Art (Cornell University Press, 1980)

—G. Picon, Modern Painting from 1800 to the Present (Newsweek Books, 1974)

—R. H. Haggar, A Dictionary of Art Terms (New Orchard Editions, Inc., 1984)

—Major European Art Movements 1900–1945 edited by Kaplan & Manso (E. P. Dutton, 1977)

—H. Read, A Concise History of Modern Painting (Praeger Publishers, 1972)

—J. Vincent, History of Art (Barnes & Noble, 1955)

—W. Sargent, The Enjoyment and Use of Color (Dover Publications, 1964)

—R. Shone, The Post-Impressionists (Gallery Books, 1979)

—World of Art series (Thames and Hudson, Ltd., 1984–1985)

1. J. Boardman, Greek Art
2. M. Wheeler, Roman Art and Architecture
3. J. Stanley-Baker, Japanese Art
4. M. Levey, From Giotto to Cezanne: A Concise History of Painting
5. W. D. Dube, The Expressionists
6. P. Pool, Impressionism
7. E. Lucie-Smith, Movements in Art Since 1945

—A Popular History of the Arts (Cavendish House, 1968)

—World Art Treasures edited by G. Hindley (Octopus Books, 1979)

—Baker & Baker, Family Treasury of Art (Galahad Books, 1981)

—Concepts of Modern Art edited by N. Stangos (Harper & Row, 1981)

—American Art Analog I, II and III compiled by M. Zellman (The Chelsea House Publishers, 1986)

—Impressionism (Chartwell Books, 1973)

—The Figure in 20th Century American Art (Selections from the Metropolitan Museum of Art, 1984)

—A Treasury of Art Masterpieces edited by T. Craven (Simon and Schuster, 1966)

—W. Gaunt, A Concise History of English Painting (Frederick A. Praeger, 1964)

—Encyclopedia of American Art (E. P. Dutton, 1981)

—D. M. Field, Great Masterpieces of World Art (The Hamlyn Publishing Group, 1979)

—The Spiritual in Art: Abstract Painting 1890–1985 (Los Angeles County Museum of Art and Abbeville Press, 1987)

—D. Piper, Looking at Art (Random House, 1984)

—The Illustrated Encyclopedia of Western Art (Exeter Books, 1979)

—Great Paintings edited by E. Mullins (St. Martin's Press, 1981)

—C. Wentinck, Masterpieces of Art: 450 Treasures of Europe (Park Lane)

—The New Painting: Impressionism 1874–1886 (The Fine Arts Museum of San Francisco, 1986)

—The Oxford Companion to Twentieth-Century Art edited by H. Osborne (Oxford University Press, 1981)

—P. Selz, Art In Our Times: A Pictorial History of 1890–1980 (Harry N. Abrams, Inc., 1981)

—McGraw-Hill Dictionary of Art edited by S. Myers (1969)

—Bearden & Henderson, Six Black Masters of American Art (Doubleday, 1972)

—ARTnews Magazine

—Art Today Magazine

Spatial qualities

art:

Form and content.

It is also distinguished by style, medium and period